Past-into-Present Series

THE UPPER CLASS

Peter Lane

Principal Lecturer in History,
Coloma College of Education

B. T. BATSFORD LTD London

First published 1972
© Peter Lane, 1972

Filmset by Keyspools Ltd, Golborne, Lancs.

Printed in Great Britain by The Anchor Press Ltd, Tiptree, Essex
for the Publishers
B. T. Batsford Ltd, 4 Fitzhardinge Street, London W1H OAH

ISBN 0 7134 1777 3

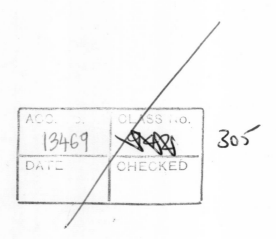

Acknowledgments

The Author and Publishers wish to thank the following for permission to reproduce the illustrations which appear in this book: Aerofilms for figs 4, 16; Camera Press for figs 54, 63; *Country Life* for fig 33; H. Felton for figs 2, 55; the Imperial War Museum for fig 62; the *Illustrated London News* for figs 13, 24, 45; the Mansell Collection for figs 22, 34, 51, 53; the National Gallery for fig 50; the National Monuments Record for figs 3, 11, 14, 15, 17, 38, 61; the National Portrait Gallery for figs 6, 7, 8, 31, 35, 39, 47, 57, 58, 60; Paul Popper for fig 64; Radio Times Hulton Picture Library for figs 1, 18, 26, 36, 37, 42, 43, 44, 48, 52, 65, 66; the Wallace Collection for fig 32; Wedgwood Ltd for fig 29.

Contents

The Illustrations

Preface

Every year about seven million people visit one or more of the stately homes of England where the upper class either used to, or still do, reside. Every day somewhere or other men either regret or look forward to being 'as drunk as a lord'. We pay to see their homes, and we pay to imitate their habits – and yet know so little about them. Not very long ago history books were written as if only the upper class had lived; lords and ladies, bishops and abbots, squires and gentlefolk were the main topics of our history books. However, things changed, and more of our history books are being written as if only the working class had lived. We have books about poverty and unions, Reform Bills and Chartism. Indeed, in some of these more recent books it is suggested that the upper class was merely a sort of parasite group which lived off the work of the lower classes.

The antics of a few members of the present-day upper class sometimes make the headlines of the popular press, which treats Lord Arran as an eccentric allowed by a generous newspaper owner to write a regular column in which he makes wild swipes at many popular changes. The same newspapers treat the Duke of Bedford as a sort of Lord Liontamer who runs a gimmicky stately home's business. All this is quite unlike the treatment given to the serious industrialist or banker who seem to be concerned with the realities of British life and its balance of payments problems. Equally, the 'peculiar' upper class is treated in a different way to the respectable, hardworking and down to earth members of the working class whose TUC conferences and wage negotiations are shown to be serious and important.

In one sense all this is almost inevitable. In the twentieth century, described by Winston Churchill as the 'age of the Common Man', the life-style and ideas of the landed upper class must sometimes appear to be irrelevant, certainly less significant. But this still does not explain why seven million people go to visit the stately homes – a far greater number than will ever trek to see Lord Stokes's British

1 The Duke of Bedford, owner of Woburn Abbey, has to work to pay off death duties (Chapter 10). Here he can be seen showing off the gold plate used only to entertain Royalty, set out in the Woburn Banqueting Room. One of his ancestors, Lord John Russell, introduced the 1832 Reform Bill into Parliament and so set in motion the progress towards democracy.

Leyland factories or the latest atomic energy station. Perhaps the visitors realise that today is built on a series of yesterdays – in which the upper class played a large part. Perhaps they realise that most of our tastes and attitudes, sports and entertainment have been adopted from the life-style of the upper classes.

In any event it cannot be denied that a class which built the stately homes, governed Britain for centuries, ruled an Empire and has managed to survive the industrial, economic and social changes of the past two hundred years, is worth some study. In these few chapters I have tried to underline some of the reasons for such a study.

Introduction

The landed gentry

Today most of us live in towns in which we get our livelihood. This is true whether we are members of the working class or of the middle class. The upper class are different to the rest of us because they are not townspeople, but country-people and landowners. Of course other people are also landowners; some people own more than one house; a few own 'a cottage and a few acres' in the country although they live and work in the town. But the upper class own hundreds or thousands of acres – and in some cases hundreds of thousands of acres.

The upper class used to get most of their income from this land (Chapter 3). Some of them farmed their own hundred or so acres, employing bailiffs, workmen and so on. The better-off members of this landed class would keep some of the land as a private park (in some cases this amounted to 3,000 acres), employ a bailiff to supervise the work of their own 'home' farm, and then parcel out the rest of the land to tenant farmers. Because they owned thousands of acres some of them were able to rent out hundreds of farms and obtained large incomes.

We will see in Chapter 6 that some of the upper class helped to make Britain the world's leading industrial power in the eighteenth and nineteenth centuries. Some, such as the Earl of Durham, had coal on their land and entered into part-nership with mine-developers and became richer as coal was dug out of their land. Others, such as the Marquess of Bute and the Duke of Westminster, watched towns grow up on their land, and earned high incomes for themselves as shops, offices, houses and factories were built on their land – which they rented out to the builders.

Income and Class

When Queen Anne offered John Churchill the title of Duke for his military services, his wife Sarah – a friend of the Queen – advised him to refuse it. 'We have neither the estate nor the income to bear a title,' she said. To overcome this hurdle, the Queen gave Churchill a pension of £5,000 a year and in 1704 gave him the royal estate of Woodstock, having persuaded Parliament to give Churchill £500,000 for the construction of his new house, Blenheim (Chapter 3, Picture 16).

Sarah Churchill, later the Duchess of Marlborough, understood the old class structure in which a titled family was a landowning family and a rich family. As we shall see, there were many cases in the fifteenth and later centuries where the family made money in one of the professions or in trade, and then bought itself an estate and a title. In recent times, Prime Minister Lloyd George (1916–22) amassed an unknown amount of money by selling titles to people who had made their fortunes in trade or industry. There were reports that there was a sort of title-catalogue going around in the early 1920s, in which each title was priced: a man could buy a viscountcy for £20,000 with lesser honours costing less.

Since the passage of the Life Peerages Act, 1958, we have had a number of peers created so that outstanding industrialists or trade union leaders, academics or former members of the House of Commons, can take an active part in the country's political life. These life peerages are different from the titles held by upper class families; the life peerage dies with its holder while the titles of the upper class families are passed on as long as there is an heir.

Title and Class

It is not true, then, that every holder of a title is a member of the upper class. Lord Stokes, who is in charge of British Leyland Motors is an industrialist and earns his money in the car industry. He is not a landowning member of the upper class. Neither is Lord George-Brown, a former member of the Labour Cabinet; he, and former trade union leaders such as Lord Ted Hill and Lord Smith, provide proof that having a title is no claim to being a member of the upper class.

On the other hand not all members of the upper class have titles. The Eden family is one of the largest landowning families in Britain. Anthony Eden was the upper class Prime Minister of the upper class Conservative Party from 1955 to 1957. One of the rewards which former Prime Ministers may claim is that of being created Earl; Clement Attlee, the former Labour Prime Minister took the title of Lord Attlee of Stepney (his former constituency); Anthony Eden took the title of the Earl of Avon. The significant point is that his family had been upper class landowners for generations without ever having had any such titles.

Titles

There are many families, such as the Edens, which are upper class yet have no titles, while today the possession of a title is no indication of a man's class. However, we should notice that most members of the upper class have been pleased to accept titles from their monarch while, until the recent past, a title was a sign that a person was a member of the upper class.

There are two broad divisions of nobility. The lower orders contain two groups. There are the *Knights*, who can put 'Sir' in front of their names and who earn for their wives the title 'Lady. . .'

Then there are the *Baronets*, a title created by James I in 1611; at first, this title was given only to men who had a clear income of £1,000 per year from land, and allowed them to write 'Sir' before their names and 'Bart' after them.

Then there is the body of peers, or upper nobility, which contains five different groups; few of the existing peerages go back before the time of William Pitt the Younger, who himself advised George III to create more than 100 new peers.

The lowest form of the peerage is the *Baron* – a title introduced into England with the Norman Conquest. At first the title was given only to people who had been given land by the king in return for performing military service. However, by the reign of Henry VI the title was being given as a reward for services rendered to the monarch and was divorced from military service. The title of *Viscount*, the fourth degree of nobility, was introduced into England in 1440 and was originally given to someone acting as an Earl's deputy.

The third degree of British nobility is conferred on an *Earl* – a title introduced during the reign of Saxon King Ethelred to indicate someone who had charge of a shire, and was a shortening of the older title of *ealdorman*. The second most important title was that of *Marquess*, or Marquis. Originally the title was given only to men who controlled frontier lands (or marches) but in 1385 Robert de Vere, then the ninth Earl of Oxford, was created a Marquess of Dublin by Richard II, and the title no longer signified a defender of the frontier.

At the top of the title tree is that of *Duke*. The first English dukedom was created by Edward III for his son – the Black Prince – who became the Duke of Cornwall. During the reign of Queen Elizabeth I, the title died out but was revived by James I who bestowed it on his favourite, George Villiers, who became the Duke of Buckingham. Since this is the highest order of nobility the title is rarely bestowed, and is a special mark of royal favour. Three of the present Dukes are members of the Royal Family.

1 Where Did They Come From?

In 1381 John Ball, a priest leader during the peasants' revolt, asked:

> When Adam dolve and Eve span
> Who was then the gentleman?

John Ball was one of the first of the English radicals who wanted a greater equality between the classes – a better life for the lower classes even if this meant that the upper class had to give up some of their economic and social privileges. Ball's use of the word 'gentleman' is important; he knew that only the upper class could be 'gentle'; the rest of the people were 'rough' from coarse, physical work.

Norman Barons

The Norman Kings were the first effective rulers of a united England, willing and able to put down rebellions whenever they occurred. But they ruled in the eleventh and twelfth centuries when communication was very poor. A ride from London to York might take as long as six days and the traveller had to contend with highwaymen, the absence of any road system, the problem of where to stay once night had fallen and how to combat the English weather.

The Norman-English Kings were also faced with the continued danger of attack from Scotland and Wales, from Ireland and the Continent. This meant that they had always to be prepared to wage war although they did not have sufficient income to pay for a regular army.

These two problems – of communication and foreign invasion – help to explain the origins of the medieval barons. The Kings divided the country into regions and appointed some of their followers to govern the various regions. These governors were given one or other of many titles – Lord, Baron, Earl, Duke – and were appointed to maintain law and order, collect taxes and to raise an army from their territory whenever called upon to do so. In return they were almost kings

2 A twelfth century Norman keep at Castle Rising. The castle was built for defence; the walls were massive, the windows small. Life inside the castle was cold and harsh by modern standards.

3 Upper class entertainment, like upper class homes, was essentially military in outlook. Here is a medieval joust.

in their own right; they had vast estates of their own which they could either keep for themselves or rent out to subordinate tenants.

In general this medieval upper class was an unlearned one; few of them could write, even fewer could read – which meant employment for many clerks and bailiffs who administered the nobleman's estate. They were also a selfish class, anxious to extend their power against that of the monarch and to safeguard what they considered their rights against any encroachment by a monarch. When they could, they used their power to force the King to make concessions so that they became even more powerful in the thirteenth and fourteenth centuries. Magna Carta was a document in which their interests were safeguarded; it is only in more recent times that this Charter has been interpreted to apply equally to non-noblemen.

Above all else, however, the medieval barons were a warlike and quarrelsome lot. Their home was a castle in which they stored their weapons and from which they sallied out to make war on a neighbour or a weak monarch, such as Stephen or John, or to join with their monarch in war against foreigners – from Scotland, Wales, the Continent or Turkey. Their main entertainment was jousting – in which they practised with the lance and the sword. They spent more money on armour than they did on non-military clothing.

The Tudors

This medieval upper class was responsible for its own decline because during the Wars of the Roses they slew each other, so that when Henry VII came to the throne there were only about twenty barons alive. Henry feared that even this small number, strengthened in time by the infant descendants of the dead barons, might be a danger to the new Tudor Monarchy. He went out of his way to weaken the old nobility while at the same time creating a new one which, he hoped, would be loyal to its creator. It is important to realise that while the upper class, like the the poor, is always with us, the membership of that class is a constantly changing one. The upper class is not a small group of families. It can best be compared to a bus – always full, but with ever different people, as first one family dies out and another climbs on board.

4 Fountains Abbey, in the West Riding of Yorkshire, was once the home of the Cistercian monks. In 1539 Henry VIII sold the estate and the Abbey to Sir Richard Gresham, one of the rising middle class who supported the Tudors.

The Reformation

Henry VIII's break with the Catholic Church led to the dissolution of the monasteries, which meant that one-third of the country's arable land was up for sale. Henry rewarded his faithful followers in his religious-political-matrimonial reform by selling off or giving away vast areas. The status-hungry courtiers were able to buy up land, which in time gave them the right to ask for titles, and, in any case, safely saw them over the barrier which divided off the town-dwelling, merchant middle class from the landed upper class. Thomas Wriothesley, for example, a lawyer, bought a number of estates in Hampshire. In 1538 he bought the house and site of Beaulieu Abbey, was created Baron Wriothesley in 1544 and Earl of Southampton in 1547. All over the country middle class men like him were busy sinking their roots in the land, converting monasteries into stately homes and founding families with titles.

This link between the new ruling class and the distribution of monastic lands is one of the reasons why successive attempts to restore Catholicism – first by Mary Tudor and later by the Stuarts – were to fail. The landed gentry feared that a restored Church might want to regain its property; they used their power to ensure the continuance of the Anglican Church and their own power. If, as someone has said, the Anglican Church is the Tory Party at prayer, it must also be said that the Church is the landed gentry at prayer.

5 Blickling Hall, Norfolk, had been a Tudor manor house where Anne Boleyn spent much of her childhood. Sir Henry Hobart, Lord Chief Justice in Charles I's reign, pulled down the old manor house and replaced it by a red-brick Jacobean house.

New upper class

Most of the new landowners had made their money in business, trade, or in one of the professions. They were more businesslike than most of the older landowners and were better able to deal with the problem that faced everyone in Tudor England – when prices began to rise very rapidly, and when personal extravagance became the rule for the upper class. Many landowners were extravagant in their buildings – William Cecil (Lord Burghley) built palaces at Burghley, Theobalds and Waltham; Lord Suffolk spent over £100,000 on a new house at Audley End; Northumberland built Syon House.

New landowners

While these extravagant tastes were being satisfied, prices were rising – so making the cost of living even higher every year. Some of the old landowners were quite unable to deal with the twin problems of having a fixed rent from their tenant farmers while, on the other hand, their costs of living were rising. This spelled ruin for many of them. But some of the old landowners, and most of the new ones, were well able to cope with these problems. By using better methods of farming, those who had their own farms found that they were selling more produce at the ever-increasing prices – and so were able to cope with their own rising cost of living. Others were prepared to change the old system of renting land; they charged a higher rent – and so obtained a higher income for themselves.

But for those who could not cope there was only one end – they were compelled to get out of the bus carrying the upper class, sell their estates to one or other of the lawyers, merchants and speculators who were trying to climb into the bus – which continued to roll on with its full complement of upper class landowners.

Heraldry

The new landowners were, like all newly-rich, very uncertain as to their position. This drove some of them to take up a new fad or craze – genealogy. The older gentry were interested in proving that their ancestry was more noble and gentler than that of the newly rich. The newly rich, on the other hand, took up genealogy in order to prove, if they could, that their ancestry was really every bit as gentle as that of the established gentry. The Tudor heralds were kept busy inventing ancestries which traced some familes back to noble times. Some new families, indeed, were not satisfied until they had traced their ancestry back to the kings of the Old Testament – the Popham family tree began with Noah seated in his Ark. Lord Burghley paid a herald to prove that his ancestry could be traced back to Owen Whyte who 'came with Harold that was Earl Godwin's son out of Cornwall'. No doubt the present-day descendants of the Earls of Essex are content

6 Robert Dudley, Earl of Leicester, was the fifth son of the Duke of Northumberland – one of the new Tudor nobility. A favourite of Elizabeth I's, a large part of his income came from his control of the salt trade – one of Elizabeth's gifts to her favourite.

7 Sir Nicolas Bacon, one of those who made their fortunes in Tudor England; Bacon was a lawyer who held many positions in the Tudor governments and so enriched himself; he was also a friend of Henry VIII's and received many former monastic estates from his grateful King. His son, Francis, became Viscount St. Albans.

with tracing their ancestry back to Tudor times; this, after all, is a long and noble line. But the Tudor Essex had to invent an ancestry for himself, rather like the Americans who try to claim that one or other of their ancestors 'came over with the Pilgrim Fathers', – unlike other Irish-American families such as the Kennedy clan, who can only trace their ancestry back to an Irish peasant farm.

The modern Englishman likes to look down on the upstart American with his wealth and extravagance, his earnest seeking after culture in Europe and his acquisition of the treasures of the Old World. Equally, the old gentry once looked down on the new. As one wrote:

> In these days he is a gentleman who is commonly taken and reputed. And whosover studieth in the universities, who professeth the liberal sciences and to be short who can live idly and without manual labour and will bear the port, charge and countenance of a gentleman, he shall be called master. . . . . And if need be, a King of Heralds shall give him for money arms newly made and invented with the crest and all: the title whereof shall pretend to have been found by the said Herald in the perusing and viewing of old registers.

Even the most powerful of the new nobility was not imune from such criticism. In 1601 a William Hansley of Market Rasen complained that 'there was none of noble blood left in the Privy Council. What are the Cecils? Are they any better than pen-gents?' and this of a family which was to give Prime Ministers until the end of the nineteenth century.

The Stuarts

If the Tudors created a new nobility, the Stuarts continued the process. Charles II sold the title of duke to pay off his debts; the Dukes of St Albans, Grafton, Richmond and Buccleuch have their origins in bastard sons of Charles II. The Earl of Sandwich got his title when he took the fleet over to the King's side at the Restoration.

The Duke of Buckingham, as Charles I's Chief Minister, handled the sale of titles for his royal master. In 1616 the money required to send an Ambassador to Paris was raised by selling two baronies for £10,000 each. In 1624 a new round of selling began to raise the £30,000 required to send Buckingham to Paris. Sales such as these went on throughout the reigns of Charles I and II.

The new rich merchants, traders and lawyers of the Stuart period, like their Tudor predecessors, were anxious to acquire landed estates and, if possible, a title as a sign that they too had managed to get onto that upper class bus. But there was more to the acquisition than mere social prestige; land was, and is, a valuable investment. Once acquired it produced its own income – as the history of the upper class shows. In the middle of the seventeenth century the Earl of Thanet had an income from his estates of £150,000 a year. Other landowners did almost as well. Men like the Earl of Westmoreland (£90,000) and the Duke of Richmond (£73,000) could afford to look down on poor nobles such as the Earl of Norwich (£3,300) and the Earl of Marlborough (£340). And while many lawyers and merchants earned similar incomes, they at least had to work for it in grubby offices and dirty towns, whereas the landowner had the income, plus the satisfaction of not having worked for it while, in addition, he had the social prestige attaching to land ownership.

Like the new Tudor nobility the new Stuart nobility was unpopular with the old. Robert Carr, the Earl of Somerset and one of James's favourites, was attacked in a ballad:

How to become a Court favourite

Let any poor lad that is handsome and young,
With parle vous France and a voice for a song,
But get on a horse and seek out good James,
He'll soon find the house, 'tis great near the Thames
It was built by a priest, a butcher by calling
But neither priesthood nor trade could keep him from falling.
As soon as you ken the pitiful loon,
Fall down from your nag as if in a swoon;
If he doth nothing more, he'll open his purse;
If he likes you ('tis known he's a very good nurse)
Your fortune is made, he'll dress you in satin,
And if you're unlearn'd he'll teach you dog Latin.

Hanoverian Upper Class

In the eighteenth century there was a new opulence as enterprising landowners developed their estates according to the latest ideas of the agrarian reformers and so earned even higher incomes, while prosperous merchants of East Indian and other companies vied with each other to spend the £100,000 required to buy a modest estate of 10,000 acres. Some, like the Duke of Chandos, started off life as minor clerks in government service but amassed sufficient from the corrupt system of the time to buy into the upper class. Others, such as Lord Hardwicke, began as lawyers and earned enough in fees to buy in. However, the most common means of acquiring an estate, or enlarging an existing one, was by a wise choice of wife. The Bedfords, the Pelhams and many other families arrived at their greatness as a result of gradual, patient, seeking-out of wives who would bring an estate or a portion of estate with them, or would bring enough of a dowry to allow the husband to buy up an addition to his estate.

Victorian Upper Class

This process of buying one's way onto the upper class bus went on through the nineteenth century. The successful leaders of industrial Britain rushed to spend fortunes on the acquisition of estates and titles. Lord Overton, a banker, bought up 30,000 acres; another banker, Evelyn Baring, became the Earl of Cromer, while mill-owners like Edward Strutt were among the first of the industrialists

8 Sir Evelyn Baring, the first Earl of Cromer, was one of the Victorian bankers and financiers who worked their way into the upper class. From 1883 to 1907 he was the virtual ruler of Egypt which had become financially bound to Britain after Disraeli's purchase of the Suez Canal shares.

to join the ranks of the landed gentry. Between 1880 and 1914 there were nearly 200 new peers, including the 'Beer Barons' – Guinness, Allsopp and Bass.

As in times past, so in the late nineteenth century the old landed gentry (itself, of course, once new but now old) considered the ostentation and extravagance of the new rich to be vulgar. When, as was often the case, the new rich were also Jews, the old rich lost little time in showing that anti-Semitism which is an unfortunate trait of theirs. Whereas the old rich gave and received the title of aristocrat, they gave the title plutocrat to the new rich such as the Rothschilds, the Sassoons and Ernest Cassel.

The class pattern which allowed the landed gentry to be the dominant members of a society is typical of most pre-industrial societies the world has ever known. Now that Britain has become an industrial society there is no room for a dominant landed gentry class. They themselves, as we shall see, have recognised this and slowly, unwillingly, but peacefully they have conceded economic, social and political power to the new classes of an industrial society.

2 At Home

The medieval baron, the first who could claim to be upper class, owed his existence to the monarch's need for an army and for someone to maintain law and order throughout the various regions of the kingdom. As an external sign of his military origins the medieval baron built a castle, which also served as a reminder to the lower classes that here was a man of power and might.

These first members of the upper class were not the 'gentle and perfect knights' that nineteenth-century poets liked to write about. On the contrary, they were a selfish and greedy crew, the bully boys of medieval England. When they faced a weak king, Stephen, they took advantage of the situation to enrich themselves, to further establish their power and to satisfy that lust for fighting which was their hall-mark.

9 Castles and royal houses of the twelfth century.

At home in the castle

Life in the castle was a hard one; the slit windows were open to the wind and rain, the open fire belched smoke into the rooms which had not yet been given chimneys. The floors were often bare earth but usually stone uncovered. The walls likewise were of stone – sometimes, but rarely, covered with tapestry.

At home in Tudor times

With the accession of Henry VII the barons were forced to give up their war-like life and by the end of the sixteenth century the upper class had begun to learn to live in restored manor houses or in new, stately homes. The Reformation put an almost complete end to the building of churches and abbeys – which had taken up most of the time of builders and craftsmen in the past. Now, in reformed England, Italian and German artists, English and French builders were employed to build and decorate town houses and country seats for the rich upper class. Penshurst and Haddon Hall were converted manor houses. Longleat, Audley End, Kenilworth and Montacute were designed in the Italian or Renaissance style. By the beginning of the seventeenth century a new profession – that of architect – had developed, with Inigo Jones as the art's first great exponent.

10 The open hearth at Penshurst Castle. There was little comfort in these castles, where even the warming fire was the source of smoke and dirt.

11 Barrington Court, Somerset. The Tudor upper class, less warlike than their predecessors, spent vast sums on building houses such as this, and equally vast sums on furnishings. With a large number of lowly-paid servants and gardeners, life for the upper class was comfortable – a far cry from life in the castle.

Sir William More spent £1,600 on the modest Losely Hall near Guildford, while Audley End was costing £190,000. Kenilworth, built as the country seat of the Earl of Leicester, cost £60,000. These prices should be set against the cost of bricks (35p per thousand in 1550) and of labour – the masons who built King's College, Cambridge, received 2½p a day in 1509.

The Tudor and Stuart upper class wanted more comfort in their homes than their medieval predecessors. Fireplaces were built to take the smoke out of the rooms being heated; glass was put into lattice windows, walls were panelled with carved wood and hung with tapestry, floors were made of polished wood and often carpeted, while houses were built with a bewildering number of rooms. Ingatestone Hall, built in 1530, had 60 rooms, including the first 'long gallery'; Woburn Abbey, designed by Inigo Jones, had 90 rooms, including 11 sitting rooms. Each of these rooms had to be suitably furnished and decorated and we read in the Earl of Cork's diary:

I have agreed with Christopher Watts, freemason and carver . . . to make me a very fair chimney, also for my parlour, which is to reach up close to the ceiling, with my coat of arms complete with crest, helmet, coronet, supporters, mantling and font-pace, which he is to set up and finish all at his own charges, fair and graceful in all respects, and for that chimney I am to pay £10, and I am to find carriage also. He is also to make twelve figures each three foot high, to set upon my staircase, for which he demands 20s. apiece and I offer him 13s.4d.

With labour and materials so cheap and with a rising number of architects and furniture makers eager to satisfy the demands of the rich upper class, the interior of the Tudor and Stuart houses took on a richer, elegant, comfortable look.

While the medieval baron had maintained a large number of armed retainers, his Tudor and Stuart successors, living in a private house and not a private castle, replaced the armed retainer with servants. Sir William Petre, living in his 60-roomed mansion, had a staff of 60 servants, costing him £250 a year, in addition to extra payments for extra servants such as messengers, carpenters, tailors and so on.

During the seventeenth century furniture-making first began to develop into a craft with styles as different as Jacobean, William and Mary, and so on. The homes of the upper class were expected to reflect these changes in fashion and many families spent a good deal in refurnishing their homes in the latest style. The men and women of the upper class were also expected to wear the latest in fashion – to be, as it were, walking reflections both of their wealth and status. Queen Elizabeth I was reputed to have had 3,000 gowns; in Stuart England there were sarcastic comments on men's fashions, with their hats, ruffs, embroidered shirts, doublets 'slashed, jagged, cut, carved, pinched and laced' and 'stuffed with four, five or six pound of bombast at the least'. Women are similarly condemned for their extravagant gowns, their ruffs 'smeared and starched in the devil's liquor', their head-dress and false hair sometimes, it appears, snipped from the head of a fair-haired child for the present of a penny. 'How much cost', complained Harrison in 1587, 'is bestowed nowadays upon our bodies, and how little upon our souls'.

Life in the new, refurnished, comfortable home is recalled in this letter written about 1660 by Sir Edward Southcote:

Dear Phil,

When you were here I intended to have given you some relation of the very grand manner of my lord grandfather's living at Standon, being there is scarce anybody but myself left that remembers it, but it went out of my mind again. . .

My lord's table was daily served with twenty dishes at a course, three courses the year about; and I remember it was brought up by twenty of his men, who, as they came up the great stairs and in the dining-room, affected to stamp louder than needed, which made a great noise like a clap of thunder every course that was brought up. My lord had every day four servants that waited behind his own chair, his gentleman, his house-steward, his chief park-keeper' and a footman to fetch to them what my lord called for; who was very curious in his wine, but Frontiniac was his favourite: but he first drank a whole quart at one draft, either of malt drink or wine and water, being advised to it by his physician as a remedy for the stone and gravel, which he was sometimes troubled with; insomuch that upon all the roads where he travelled, either into Staffordshire, or to us in Surrey, all the inns where he used to lodge kept a glass that held a quart, called 'My Lord Aston's Glass'. I saw one of them at the 'Altar Stone' at Banbury not many years ago.

12 The white drawing-room in Houghton Hall, Norfolk. In the eighteenth century the upper class employed one of the members of the new profession (architects) to build new houses and redesign old ones. Statesmen like Robert Walpole, the owner of Houghton Hall, used the corrupt political system to enrich themselves and spent some of their new wealth on homes such as Houghton.

Hanoverian comforts

The Georgian upper class had several advantages over their Stuart forefathers. The professions of architect and furniture designer had grown and become even more sophisticated; the rich had grown accustomed to living in style and opulence which had been a novelty for some of their fathers, and their expectations of what was grand or upper class were even greater and grander. One of the hallmarks of the upper class has always been lavish expenditure. One is reminded of the Rolls Royce advertisement: 'If you have to ask the price, then this car isn't for you.' The upper class have never had to ask the price of anything – they have always spent as Robert Walpole did when he built a palace for himself at Houghton in Norfolk. The house took thirteen years to build and involved moving a whole village which detracted from the view. Kent designed the furniture and decoration, Rysbrach the chimney pieces and statuary, while Europe was scoured to find the pictures to adorn the walls. The cost is unknown but must have approached that of Audley End (£190,000). Walpole was also building the Old Lodge at Richmond Park (£14,000) and renting a London House in Arlington Street for £300 a year. The upkeep of all these houses was enormous; at Houghton he employed 77 weeders in the gardens, his wine bill was £1,000 a year and his personal expenditure between 1714 and 1718 was £90,000.

A staff of 50–70 was common for the great landlords, in addition to outside gardeners and gamekeepers. The Duke of Dorset, living at Knole, paid his 45 servants £474 a year. A total bill of £1,000 a year was not uncommon by the end of the century, with a hierarchy of earnings from £100 a year for the house steward, £60 for the clerk of the kitchen, £43 for the head keeper, £40 for the head cook, £28 for the housekeeper, down to £8 for footmen and £4 for maids: board, lodging and livery were, of course, supplied, and in some kitchens a supply of cold meat, tea and punch was always on the table. The upkeep of such establishments was equally enormous. In 1736 the Duke of Kingston stayed at his Thoresby home for only 3 months but the food bill came to £1,477.

For the rich, life was pleasant, but again we have to be on our guard. The Victorian poets and pre-Raphaelite painters have misled some into thinking that every medieval baron was a Sir Lancelot-like 'sweet and gentle knight'. We know that this was far from the case. Equally, we may make the mistake of thinking that the eighteenth-century members of the upper class, in their beautiful houses staffed with armies of servants and decorated with the most beautiful furniture and paintings, would have been affected by their surroundings and been the gentle, sophisticated, polite beings that the surroundings called for. In fact this was not so. Fielding's Squire Western, who spent all the morning in the hunting field and all the evening with drinking companions, retiring to bed 'so drunk that he could not see', was, according to contemporary accounts, typical of his age and class. Drunkenness was the national vice of all Englishmen and the upper-class gentleman boasted of being a 'four bottle a day man' when he could, in fact, drink his four bottles of spirits each day. Even as late as 1784 François de la Rochefoucauld, on a visit to the Duke of Grafton, wrote 'Very often I have heard things mentioned in good society which would be in the grossest taste in France. The sideboard too is furnished with a number of chamber-pots and it is a common practice to relieve oneself whilst the rest are drinking; one has no kind of concealment and the practice strikes me as most indecent.'

The English upper class had yet to acquire that veneer of manners and standard of behaviour which marked off the French upper class.

Victorian homes

The nineteenth-century members of the upper classes seemed determined to spend even more lavishly than their forefathers had done. Although wages were

13 A banquet at Alnwick Castle on the coming-of-age of Lord Warkworth, the son of the Duke of Northumberland. As befitted the owner of the largest house in the possession of a private person, the Duke entertained on a vast scale.

higher, and materials dearer than they had been in, say, the eighteenth century, it is still worthwhile remembering that skilled craftsmen were only earning £2 a week when, between 1852 and 1866 the Duke of Northumberland reconstructed his Alnwick castle at a cost of £320,000. This was the largest house in the possession of a private person, but cost less than Fonthill Abbey (£400,000) and only a little more than the Marquess of Ailesbury's Tottenham House, Wiltshire, which cost £250,000. Many country seats underwent nineteenth century face-lifts, and central heating, gas lighting, hydraulic lifts and other amenities were added to make the stately homes more comfortable.

The annual expenditure of an upper-class family depended of course on its income and life-style. In 1914 the Earl of Derby was still spending £50,000 a year, and when the King and Queen stayed at his house, Knowsley, for the Grand National, over 40 guests and their 120 servants were entertained. The Earl of Lonsdale kept a private orchestra of 25 musicians as part of his establishment. The essential requirements for the great household in the nineteenth, as in any other, century was the lavish provision of domestic servants. The indoor and outdoor staff of a peer would number from about 20 up to perhaps 80 or 100, and there was a fairly widely accepted scale of provision according to income, defined by *The Complete Servant* (1825) as 4 females and 3 men at an income of £1,000 to £1,500 a year, rising to 11 females and 13 men at £4,000 to £5,000 a year. At the latter income it was suggested that servants should take £1,250 a year, or 25 per cent of income, household expenses £1,666 (33 per cent), clothes £1,250 and rent

26

£625, the latter presumably for a town house for the season. Servants were a major and increasing expense throughout the century, as wages rose and men, in particular, revolted against the long hours and drudgery of life 'below stairs'. Already in 1870 a writer was complaining that 'Servants are becoming scarce, wages are rising, and the work performed is not so well done as it used to be'. In the mid-eighteenth century a maid could be employed for £6·50 to £10 a year, a footman for £15 and a valet for £25, but by the time of Mrs Beeton's 1888 edition a 'general' maid's wages were specified as £10 to £16, a cook's at £20 and a valet's at £35 plus.

Town houses

Reference has been made several times to the London or town house which many of the upper classes kept. While the possession of a landed estate and a country seat was the absolute necessity for membership of the upper class, many of them also wanted to retain their political and social contacts with the Court and London life. This had been so in Tudor England, when the Strand contained the houses of Essex and other noblemen. In the eighteenth century the aristocracy moved into Mayfair and built Hanover and Berkeley Squares. Here and there were the palatial houses of the great aristocrats – Devonshire House, between Piccadilly and south Berkeley Square, Lansdowne House, and Grosvenor House containing the Duke of Westminster's art collection. Charles II built himself a palace in Chelsea (now Chelsea Hospital) and nearby the Duke of Beaufort built a sumptuous house, now the site of Beaufort Street. The Duke of Wellington, at Apsley House, and Lord Palmerston, lower down the road in Piccadilly, had only a short journey to make from their London homes to the countryside which began at Marble Arch.

Open house

And now these town houses have all been sold off. Rootes, the car firm, built a huge showroom on the site of the Duke of Devonshire's house – a symbol of the emergence of a new society. Offices, clubs, property companies have each in

14 The Library, Easton Neston, Northants. One of the well furnished, beautifully designed rooms in one of the upper class homes.

15 Penshurst Place, the birthplace of Sir Philip Sidney, whose father was given the house by Edward VI in 1552. It is an outstanding example of the manor house owned by the upper classes.

their turn taken over the former homes of the upper class who retreated to their country seats. Even these, however, are no longer 'theirs' in quite the same way. Increased taxes, higher wages and rising prices have all contributed to make life more difficult for the upper classes. Many of them have now entered upon a new era by presenting the British public and tourists with a chance to visit their stately homes, at a price. This, however, is no new idea. In the eighteenth century there was a recognised 'Grand Tour' of English country houses and famous homes such as Holkham and Wilton, Blenheim and Chatsworth were open to the public on fixed days. The owner of Stourehead built an inn to accommodate visitors. In 1778 Lord Lyttleton complained: 'Coaches full of travellers of all denominations, and troupes of holiday neighbours, are hourly chasing me from my apartment or strolling about the environs keeping me prisoner in it. The lord of the place can never call it his during the finest part of the year.' Today's landed gentry, led by the enterprising Lord Montagu, have a different view of the visitor; in their 'School for stately home owners' run by Lord Montagu they are taught how to attract more visitors and to make the visit worthwhile so that they can expect a return sometime in the future. Far from being a nuisance, the visitor is now regarded as essential.

3 Down on the Farm

Sometimes people ask 'How can you tell whether a family belongs to the upper class as distinct from the rich middle class?' There are a number of answers which might help. But one mark has always distinguished the upper from the middle class which is essentially a town class, depending on trade, business or one of the professions for its income. The upper class is above all a landowning class, a country class with its roots in the countryside from which it derives its income.

Medieval landowners

The medieval barons, the first of our upper class, were given their land by a monarch who realised that he needed the help of some of his followers if law and order was to be maintained. Later entrants into the bus carrying the upper class through history acquired the land which marked them out as having qualified for membership of this class – by war, by gifts from a Tudor or Stuart monarch, or by

16 Blenheim Palace, a gift from the nation to the Duke of Marlborough after his victories against Louis XIV. The estate, like all upper class estates, was part massive home, part park and part farmland rented out for income.

purchase, so that middle class money bought from a debt-ridden member of the upper class that land which the latter could no longer afford to keep. Thus does the bus lose some of its passengers while others climb on.

The medieval baron, who provided the King with an army when required, used some of the land for his own benefit – as a pleasure park where he hunted, fished and shot, and also ran his own farm with the aid of a bailiff supervising the work of various members of the lower classes such as milkmaids and ploughmen. The rest of the medieval baron's land was rented out to different members of the lower classes; some were rich tenant farmers, others might have had only an acre or two, while others would have only the cottage in which they lived, and a small garden of their own.

These medieval manors were carried on for profit – they had to be, since the baron had to get enough from the land to maintain himself and his family, as well as contribute to the monarch's army when required.

The manorial rolls give us the details of how the estates were run. On one estate the villeins each hold half a 'virgate' of land (12 to 15 acres), for which they must plough, sow and till half an acre of the lord's land and give such other services as are required by the bailiff, pay a quarter of seed-wheat at Michaelmas, a peck of wheat, 4 bushels of oats and 3 hens on 12 November, and at Christmas a cock, 2 hens and twopennyworth of bread: there are also some cash payments – a half-penny on 12 November and a penny whenever they brew. Each villein is also to reap 3 days at harvest time, but for this he is to have ale and a loaf of bread, and is entitled to carry home as large a sheaf of corn as he can lift on his sickle. On another manor at Ibstone in Buckinghamshire lives a privileged freeholder who holds his virgate by charter and pays only 1d yearly at Christmas: his further liability, however, is to ride with his lord whenever there is war between England and Wales, to be armed with iron helmet, breastplate and lance, and to remain with him at his own expense for 40 days. Besides villeins, there are also at Ibstone a number of inferior cottars who, for their small holdings of a few acres, pay a rent of from 1s 2d to 2s a year, and are required to work only a few days at hay-making and harvest: for the rest of the year they are free labourers, available to be hired by the lord or by more prosperous villeins.

Tudor landowners

We have already seen that during the fifteenth and sixteenth centuries this country experienced the first of the bouts of inflation with which modern Englishmen are familiar. This inflation created problems for some Tudor landowners who were receiving a fixed rent from their tenants but found that they in turn had to pay ever-increasing prices for food, furniture, building, etc. For some, the difference between their fixed income and their rising expenditure proved to be an insoluble problem; these were the landowners who sold out to the successful traders and businessmen, lawyers and courtiers who were anxious to obtain land as a ticket into the upper class.

17 Gorhambury, the country seat of the Earl of Veralum – the descendant of Francis Bacon. In the grounds are the ruins of Francis Bacon's mansion.

These new landowners, and some of the older ones, were more practical-minded than the failures had been. One such new man was Nicolas Bacon. The son of a sheep-reeve of the monastery of Bury St Edmunds, Nicolas had the advantage of birth in the prosperous farming country of East Anglia: other examples of social mobility from the same area include Wolsey and Gardiner, the children respectively of a butcher and a cloth-maker. After studies at Cambridge and Gray's Inn, Bacon received his first appointment as solicitor to the Court of Augmentations in 1537 at a salary rising from £10 to £70 a year: 9 years later he was promoted to attorney to the Court of Wards at £90 a year, and after 12 years more to the altogether different status of Lord Keeper at £1,200 a year. By the end of his life his total income from offices and lands was not less than £5,500 a year. Throughout his career Bacon consistently bought land as and when he could, and during the 20 years of his Keepership his annual expenditure on it amounted to £1,380. By the end he had bought £40,000 worth of property, including 30 manors and 3 country houses, Redgrave Hall, Gorhambury Hall and Stiffkey Hall.

Bacon and his fellow travellers brought to their land the same ability which they had used as lawyers or traders. They had no compunction about raising the rents of their tenants:

A Prayer for Landlords issued in the reign of Edward VI began, 'O Lord, we pray thee that the landlords may not rack and stretch out the rents.' The most constant complaint in Tudor England was the inflation of rents and the heavy 'fine' or 'gressom' imposed on an incoming tenant for entry into a copyhold or

31

renewal of a lease for a term of years. The gressom was by custom, though not by law, generally limited to 2 years rent, but to raise this, or the rent itself, was the most obvious way for landowners to protect themselves against rising costs and prices. Nor was it necessarily unjust that a tenant-farmer who was receiving substantially higher profits from the sale of corn and meat should be expected to pay more for his holding.

Others of the new landowners farmed an increasing part of their own estates, and enclosed land for sheep and arable farming. Sir Richard Gresham, the Tudor merchant and financier, paid £11,000 for Fountains Abbey (Chapter 1, Picture 3) and proceeded to increase the profit on this estate from five per cent to fifteen per cent per year. Sheep-farming, which brought a profit of from £3·60 to £5 per 'long hundred' (120) in the 1540s, was yielding about £14 in the 1620s; from this it does not seem that the sheep-farmer had much to fear from inflation.

The Agrarian Revolution

In the eighteenth century England began to experience the first stages of the Industrial and Agrarian Revolutions which, in time, changed the face of the

18 Thomas Coke (of Holkham) the first Earl of Leicester, one of the leaders in the Agrarian Revolution of the eighteenth century.

19 One of the signs of the decreasing power of the upper class was the Repeal of the Corn Laws in 1846. Cobden persuaded Peel, leader of the upper class Conservative Party, to accept the arguments of the Anti-Corn Law League.

country – and were to lead to the decline of the upper class. But the agrarian improvements that have earned the title 'Agrarian Revolution' were pioneered and developed by the rich upper classes who were anxious to increase their incomes and able to afford the capital investment that the new methods required.

One of the main features of this period of agrarian change was the continued enclosure of vast areas of the countryside. Sometimes this was done by a simple agreement between the parties concerned; more often, after 1760, the method used was for the various landowners and tenants to apply for an Act of Parliament.

On their larger, enclosed farms the landowners required fewer workers, could afford to buy the new machinery and, having increased the productivity both of their land and their workpeople, saw their incomes increasing. Coke of Holkham, perhaps the most successful of the eighteenth-century improvers, raised the rentals on his Norfolk estates from £2,200 to £20,000 a year within 40 years. The average rent in Arthur Young's time was 50p an acre compared with $2\frac{1}{2}$p in the Middle Ages, and the average cost of land $33\frac{1}{2}$ years' rent instead of 20. Profits ranged from 14–20 per cent a year.

Corn Law repeal

These prosperous landowners controlled the political system (Chapter 4) and used their power to get Parliament to pass the Corn Laws (1815). But throughout

33

20 Disraeli had prophesied ruin for the British farmer after the repeal of the Corn Laws (Picture 19). However, it was the combination of bad weather and cheap American wheat which finally ruined the British farmer in the 1870s. The American farmer in the cartoon doesn't want to be blamed for the bad weather, although he agrees that he is responsible for the cheap wheat being imported into Britain.

the nineteenth century the political power of the upper class was gradually eroded as first the middle-class industrialists and later the skilled workmen were given the vote (Chapter 4). It is one of the truths of politics that 'whoever has the power uses it for his own benefit'; the landed upper class had used their power to pass Corn Laws and Game Laws. When the middle class got a share in this political power they used it to force Parliament to repeal the Corn Laws (1846). The landed class were opposed to such a change but, as the Prime Minister of the Conservative government wrote to the Whig leader, Lord John Russell (a son of the Duke of Bedford), 'there are many peers who, whatever their opinions might be about the Corn Laws, would be anxious that any measure which passed the House of Commons should pass the House of Lords, and would do all they could to assist it.'

Disraeli led a small group of Conservatives in opposition to the majority of the Conservative MPs and Lords who followed Peel's example and voted for the repeal of the Corn Laws. He prophesied the decline of the landowner as foreign food flooded into this country, and he also foresaw the continued rise of the urban, industrial interest and the corresponding decline of the landed, aristocratic interest. For about twenty years his prophecy seemed a foolish one; British farmers had no difficulty in selling their products at ever rising prices to the growing and ever richer populations of the industrial towns. The development of the railway system meant that food could be transported to hitherto inaccessible parts of the country; new scientific methods of farming helped the landed class to continue to enjoy high rents.

Agrarian depression

But in the early 1870s British agriculture entered a period of depression which was to last until the middle of this century. In ten years the price of wheat fell by half while the price of mutton and beef fell by about one-third. The reason for this fall was the influx of imports of wheat from America, where rents were lower; the use of machinery on very large farms helped to keep costs down. The development of the railway and the steamship had brought the grains of Mid-Western America within a week's journey of the mass markets of the United Kingdom. The development of refrigation led to massive imports of frozen beef from Argentina and of frozen mutton from Australia and New Zealand. The depression hit the arable estates much more than the pastoral, the south and east of the country much more than the north and west. For nearly all landowners it meant considerable reductions in rent to their tenants and, hence, reduced incomes. On an average, agricultural rents fell by one-quarter between 1870 and 1914, most of the fall being concentrated into the years 1875–90; on some arable lands rent-reductions of 50 per cent were common, and in one extreme case 638 acres at Steeple, in Essex, which in 1873 paid £760 in rent, had to be rented for a mere £1 a year between 1886 and 1891.

The end of the farming upper class

It is significant that many of the new rich of the late nineteenth century did not buy huge estates as their Tudor and Stuart predecessors had done; it was also worthy of note that many of the old families were forced to begin to economise, to seek profits on the Stock Exchange and to begin to play a larger part in the industrial life of the country. Disraeli's prophecy that the landed interest would decline was now proving to be true.

Until 1851 more than half the people in England lived in small villages, earning their living directly or indirectly through agriculture. In these villages the people of all classes shared many common interests; they worshipped at the same Church, took part in the same local events, met each other frequently and were known to each other in a way that is impossible in a large industrial town. While each individual in the village knew that there was a social hierarchy, with the landed nobleman at the top and the poor peasant at the bottom, with each person having his own known and accepted place in the structure, there was less danger of a class war in these villages than there was in an industrial town where the classes

35

21 An idealised picture of life in the village. Harvest Home was only one of the occasions on which the entire village from the squire to the lowest labourer met together and shared a common life.

live and worship, play and shop in quite distinct East (or poor) and West (or rich) ends of the town or city.

In 1755 Jean Rouquet noted: 'The Englishman always has in his hands an accurate pair of scales in which he scrupulously weighs up the birth, the rank, and above all the wealth of the people he meets, in order to adjust his behaviour towards them accordingly.' This was not the case in Russia or France, Spain or Italy – but was exactly the case in Ireland where the English landowners treated the native Irish in a way they never have dreamt of using in their own English estates. If we want to know why there were revolutions on the Continent and not in England, why the Irish waged continual war against their landowners, whereas the English peasantry rarely did so, the answer lies in the way in which the English landowner lived and treated his subjects as compared with the way his European counterparts behaved to their inferiors.

In the twentieth century the landed upper class have continued to find life very difficult. Many of them are reluctant to give up their estates but find it equally difficult to make them pay. One of the ways in which some of them have tried to make ends meet is by opening their homes to the paying public, and as we saw in Chapter One, an ever-increasing number of us seem to want to pay to see how the rich man used to live.

4 The Ruling Class

Medieval rulers

We have already seen that the original members of the upper class, the medieval barons, owed their very existence to the monarch's inability to rule the country without their help. In return for their landed estates they ensured that law and order were maintained, taxes collected, criminals captured and punished. Unfortunately there is a tendency for power to corrupt, and many of the upper class became selfish tyrants, anxious to extend their own power and to use it for their own interests. Even in Magna Carta they had no interest in the rights of any of the King's poorer subjects.

Tudor rulers

The new monarchy started by Henry VII was anxious to contain the power of the barons. One of the main characteristics of the upper class was to give their servants a distinctive uniform – rather like jockeys today carry an owner's colours, so did these servants. A very rich landowner would have, in effect, a private army which could be used to frighten judges and juries, King's messengers and local people. Henry VII was the first to bring in effective legislation aimed at cutting these armies down to size. The Statutes of Livery and Maintenance (1494 and 1504) forbade the use of distinctive livery and uniforms, and any offenders were

22 A view of the Court of Wards in Elizabeth I's reign. The new Tudor monarchy depended on lawyers such as these, and in return the lawyers enriched themselves. (See Chapter 1, Picture 7.)

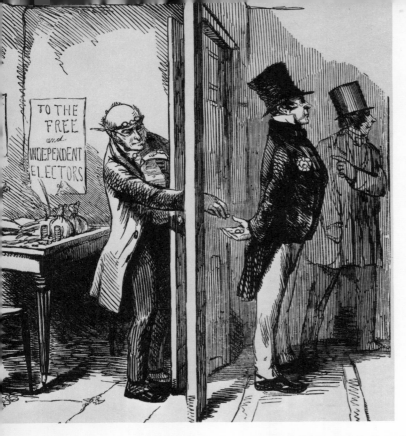

23 One view of the corrupt electoral system, 1853. The upper class controlled this system and used it for their own benefit.

to be tried at the King's Court or Star Chamber – and not at a local court where they might overawe the judge and jury. Francis Bacon recalled how Henry VII had been vigilant to see that these laws were kept:

'There remaineth to this day a report that the king was on a time entertained by the Earl of Oxford (that was his principal servant for both war and peace) nobly and sumptuously at his Castle at Henningham [Hedingham]. And, at the king's going away, the Earl's servants stood, in a seemly manner, in their livery-coats, with cognizances, ranged on both sides, and made the king a lane. The king called the earl unto him and said:

"My lord, I have heard much of your hospitality, but I see that it is greater than the speech. These handsome gentlemen and yeomen which I see on both sides for me are sure your menial servants."

The Earl smiled, and said:

'It may please your grace, that were not for mine ease. They are most of them my retainers that are come to do me service at such a time as this, and chiefly to see your grace."

The king started a little, and said:

"By my faith, my lord, I thank you for my good cheer, but I may not endure to have my laws broken in my sight. My attorney must speak with you."

And it is part of the report that the Earl compounded for no less than 15,000 marks.'

Hanoverian Rulers

In both Tudor and Stuart England the monarchs relied on the upper class to help them in governing of the country. The peers and their sons controlled the political life of the nation.

In 1793 a *Report on the State of representation* found that over half of the MPs were returned by one or other kind of patron – '... Your committee report, that the gross defects and abuses which ... they have proved to exist in the present mode of representation, have established a system of private patronage, which renders the condition of the House of Commons practically as follows.

```
71  Peers and the Treasury nominate ........  92
         Procedure the return of .............  77
                                                 ──
         Patronage of 71 peers and the Treasury    169
91  Commoners nominate ..............  82
         Procedure the return of..............  57
                                                 ──
         Patronage of 91 commoners              139
162  return ...............  308 out of 513 members ......
```

Nineteenth-century rulers

In the nineteenth century the face of England changed, as first the steam engine led to the development of a factory system, then the railway system aided the rapid growth of new industries and larger towns and finally, the development of the steamship brought England into closer contact with the outside world so that a world economy had begun to replace the national economies by 1914. The growth of many industries led to the creation of the new, rich, industrial middle class who fought a constant unarmed war against the old upper class. In 1832 they won one battle when the upper class were forced to give up their monopoly of political power; in 1846 the middle class gained another victory when the Corn Laws were repealed and the upper class lost a monopoly in providing England's growing population with food; in 1888 a Conservative government ended the upper class control of local government when it created the system of County Councils which has lasted until to-day.

And yet even in 1900, nine of the nineteen members of the Cabinet sat in the House of Lords where the Prime Minister, Robert Arthur Talbot Gascoyne Cecil, ninth Earl and third Marquess of Salisbury, continued the family habit of helping the monarch to govern. William Hansley may have complained 'What are the Cecils? Are they any better than pen-agents?' By 1900 the Cecils, like so many of the once newly-rich, seemed to be permanent members of the traditional upper, ruling class. Other members of the Cabinet were the Marquess of Lansdowne whose great-grandfather had been Prime Minister under George III, and the Duke of Devonshire who owned one hundred and eighty-six thousand acres in eleven counties.

24 A dinner given by the Marchioness of Londonderry to 3,000 pitmen in the grounds of her home at Seaham Hall. Many members of the Victorian upper class had invested in the industrial revolution and so increased their family wealth. At this time, 1857, the miners did not have a vote. In the twentieth century the miners of Seaham elected Ramsay MacDonald as their MP; he became the first Labour Prime Minister.

Paternal rulers

One of the characteristics of this ruling class was their use of their power. Many of the more notable social reforms of the century owed much to the activities of reforming Lords such as Shaftesbury and Althorp. The aristocracy understood the meaning of *noblesse oblige*; they understood that with power came responsibility. They were very conscious of their position. When Lord Herbert of Cherbury was shipwrecked at Dover in 1609 he leaped into the only rescue boat, used his drawn sword to prevent anyone but Sir Thomas Lucy from entering, and then deserted the sinking ship and its crew and made for the safety of the shore – an action which he was not ashamed to record in his autobiography. In the nineteenth century they expected to live in an atmosphere of forelock tugging and gaping servility. Lord Rosslyn was not the only member of this class who thought that, while his Christian duty was to look after his dependents, 'those who served had no right to an opinion'.

But while they expected to be obeyed, the upper class did realise that they had their duties – to look after their dependents as Lord Rosslyn put it. In 1834 Charles Greville was staying at Petworth and attended Lord Egremont's open-air feast for the poor of the neighbourhood:

'A fine sight it was, fifty-four tables, each fifty feet long, were placed in a vast semi-circle on the lawn before the house. The tables were all spread with cloths and plates and dishes: two great tents were erected in the middle to receive the provisions which were conveyed in carts, like ammunition. Plum puddings and boiled and roast beef were spread out, while hot joints were prepared in the kitchen and sent forth as soon as the firing of guns announced the hour of the feast. Tickets were given to the inhabitants of a certain district, and the number was about four thousand; but, as many more came, the old Peer could not endure that there should be anybody hungering outside his gates, and he went out himself and ordered the barriers to be taken down and admittance given to all. They think six thousand were fed.'

A band paraded through the grounds while the people, dressed in their best clothes, tucked in ravenously. In the evening ten thousand people were treated to a firework display, and the enjoyment of the crowds was eclipsed by the satisfaction of the earl:

'There was something affecting in the contemplation of that old man – on the verge of the grave – rejoicing in the diffusion of happiness and finding keen gratification in relieving the distresses and contributing to the pleasures of the poor.'

Almsgiving of this sort was widespread. In the mid-nineteenth century it was normal for between four and seven per cent of the income of an estate to be paid out in charities. Some, like Lord Montagu of Beaulieu, built schools for the children of the estate; others built houses and paid the salaries for district nurses or doctors.

Concessionary rulers

One of the ways in which the English upper class differs from their European cousins is that they have always been prepared after a long struggle to give up some of their powers when a sufficiently large volume of demand has been made.

25 *A feast in the grounds of Ham House, Surrey,* painted by Rowlandson.

26 (*Left*) The Reform Bill of 1832 receiving the royal assent. The Bill was steered through Parliament by one of the most aristocratic Cabinets of the nineteenth century.

27 (*Right*) One view of Disraeli's action in passing the Second Reform Act, 1867. The upper class look on in fear as their leader, Disraeli, takes Britannia through a hedge marked 'Reform'. Some of the upper class, including a future Prime Minister, Lord Salisbury, realised that on the other side of the hedge lay democracy, the age of the common man and the end of rule by the upper class.

In 1828 the Prime Minister was the Duke of Wellington. When there was a danger of civil war in Ireland after Daniel O'Connell had been illegally elected MP for Clare, Wellington persuaded the Tories to give up one of their longstanding principles and remove the penalties which prevented Catholics from enjoying the full liberty enjoyed by others.

In 1832 the Reform Bill was carried by one of the most aristocratic Cabinets of the century. Lord Grey, the Prime Minister, set out to show that 'in these days of democracy it is possible to find real capacity in the high aristocracy'. There were only three commoners in his Cabinet which passed the Bill which spelt the end of the political power previously enjoyed by their class. Most aristocrats resented this betrayal, but few were prepared to go as far as the Duke of Buckingham, who brought his cannon ashore from his yacht to fight reform.

It was an aristocratic Cabinet of Tories which piloted the repeal of the Corn Laws through the Commons and a reluctant Wellington who persuaded sufficient of his fellow-Lords to pass the measure through the Upper House. In 1867 it was a Conservative government which passed the first Reform Act giving votes to working men – which, in time, was to lead to the formation of the Labour Party, the increasing radicalism of the Liberal Party and, as Lord Salisbury foresaw, 'doomed the aristocratic principle'.

28 The last source of upper class political power was the House of Lords which came under attack in the late nineteenth and early twentieth centuries from the Irish (Redmond), Labour and Liberal Parties. The noble Lord in the cartoon, entitled *A Near Miss*, was wrong; in 1911 the Parliament Act effectively ended the system by which the House of Lords was equal to the House of Commons. After 1911 the country was ruled by the Commons, which was elected by the middle and lower classes.

Still there

The English upper class did not suffer the fate of their French and Russian cousins who resisted change until the pressure of demand for reform grew into a revolutionary tide which swept them away. In England the upper class conceded – and retained their position. But by the beginning of the twentieth century this position was obviously a different one from that which they had enjoyed in 1800. The increasing democratisation of the political system, the end of their domination of local politics and the onset of the agricultural depression of the 1870s forced many of the upper class to look again at what was happening to them. Between 1909 and 1911 the upper class faced the Radical Liberal government led by Asquith, who had Lloyd George as his Chancellor. Lloyd George, anxious to increase the amount spent on social reform and national defence, thought that the upper class was the one class which should be taxed even more rigorously than hitherto. Higher death duties, increased income tax and the imposition of super-tax, plus the threat of a land tax, all affected the net incomes of the upper class. Having resisted the passage of the Budget through the Commons where they were led by Salisbury's nephew, Balfour, the upper class looked to the House of Lords

43

as the last bastion of their class. In 1909 the Lords rejected the budget – and in so doing challenged the whole principle of democratic government. As the Liberals pointed out in the subsequent election in January 1910 the country had to choose whether it was to be governed by 'The Peers or the People'. In spite of the activities of a small minority of die-hards, the majority of the Lords, representing the upper class realised that democracy had come to stay and in 1911 voted for the Liberal's Parliament Bill which effectively ended the real political power previously enjoyed by their class. Even so, the Bill was drafted by a Cabinet which contained one baron, one viscount, three earls and a marquis, while the Home Secretary – Winston Churchill – was the grandson of a duke.

5 The Serving Class

Confident Upper Class

Prince Leopold of Loewenstein married the daughter of the publisher, Victor Gollancz and in 1970 wrote a biography of his late wife. The Prince compared the attitudes of his father and class with those of the Jewish publisher who was his father-in-law. The Prince noted that the wealth which his family had always enjoyed had given him a carefree and detached outlook on life. He and his class never had to worry about 'What shall we eat?' or 'What shall we drink?' or 'Wherewithal shall we be clothed?' He remembered that when he had been eighteen he had asked his father 'What do you think I should take up as a career; what do you want me to become?' His father exploded: 'What do you mean "become"? You don't have to *become* anything; you are; is that not enough?'

From medieval times the nobleman's child grew up enjoying a life of comfort and leisure, living in a country house with a large income earned from farming profits and supported by a huge number of servants. One might expect such children to grow up selfish, lazy and concerned only for themselves. In fact, the upper class had a view of life which drove them to spend a good deal of time serving the State – for nothing – as Justices of the Peace or looking after the poor. From an early age they learned to offer generous hospitality to everyone while, at the

29 The Wedgwood family painted by Stubbs in 1780. The founder of the Wedgwood firm (seated with his wife on the right of the picture) had made enough money for his family to live like the upper class.

30 Music at home – for those who had homes of this size.

same time, clearly understanding the distinctions between their own upper class and every other class. While they admired the learning of tutors and the ability of artists and inventors, they always understood and showed that they understood that such middle class people were their inferiors. They grew up confident that their class was superior and that the social divisions in society would always remain. They accepted as God-given the inequality of opportunity which an accident of birth had given them and equally they accepted that while they should care for their inferiors and dependants, there was little – if anything – that could be done about the grinding poverty in which most of these lower orders lived, nor was there any point in their trying to make the divisions of wealth any fairer or more equal.

In all this they grew up with a different view of life from that which inspired the capitalist middle class which became more important from the seventeenth century onward, and which finally overwhelmed the upper class in the late nineteenth century. The capitalist class believed in self-improvement; a middle class father would have had a different answer to the question: 'What do you want me to become?' The middle class had a strong belief in self-help and had little of the upper class's idea of looking after dependants; if a factory owner had to sack 500 men so that their families suffered, he never considered that he had any responsibility to these members of a lower class.

Social divisions

To the tune *All Things Bright and Beautiful* the upper class and their social inferiors sang

> The rich man in his castle,
> The poor man at the gate
> God made them high and lowly
> And ordered their estate.

The upper class realised that if God had ordered their estate He had also imposed on each different estate certain obligations; the lower had to obey – indeed to echo – the words:

> God bless the squire and his relations,
> And keep us all in our proper stations.

Nevertheless, the upper class had to use their power for the benefit of the community as a whole. Certainly they had to use it for their own benefit – they were not social revolutionaries! But they had also to use their power for the benefit of the lower orders. They understood the meaning of the phrase *noblesse oblige* – that power had its responsibilities. In the 1930s the Prime Minister, Stanley Baldwin, was under attack from the newspapers owned by Lords Rothermere and Beaverbrook. Baldwin accused the Press of using their power (to influence opinion, to attack without any danger of being attacked in the Press which they owned). He accused them of behaving as if their power did not impose on them any sense of responsibility. In a famous phrase, Baldwin accused them of acting as if power had no responsibility 'the prerogative of the harlot throughout the ages'. Although there have been exceptions, it is fair to say that the upper class had accepted the responsibilities that have gone with power whereas, in general, the middle class have behaved with little sense of responsibility.

In 1838 Charles Greville, the diarist, explained this tradition of public service allied with an acceptance of social power:

> The Duke of Rutland is as selfish a man as any of his class – that is, he never does what he does not like, and spends his whole life in a round of such pleasures as suit his taste, but he is neither a foolish nor a bad man, and partly from a sense of duty, partly from inclination, he devotes time and labour to the interest and welfare of the people who live on his estate. He is a guardian of a very large union, and he not only attends regularly the meetings of the Poor Law Guardians every week or fortnight, and takes an active part in their proceedings, but he visits those paupers who receive out-of-doors relief, sits and converses with them, invites them to complain to him if they have anything to complain of, and tells them that he is not only their friend but their representative at the Assembly of Guardians, and that it is his duty to see that they are nourished and protected.

Social reformers.

The upper class led the demand for a social reform in the nineteenth century. One eminent reformer was Anthony Ashley Cooper, the seventh Earl of Shaftesbury. At the age of twenty-seven he wrote in his diary: 'On my soul, I believe that I desire the welfare of mankind.' At eighty-four years of age he said, of his approaching death: 'I cannot bear to leave the world with all the misery in it.'

On another occasion he visited a school for poor children who told him that they were cold and hungry. He asked the middle class superintendent of the school: 'What can we do for them?'

'My God shall supply all their need,' replied the superintendent with easy faith.

'Yes,' said Lord Shaftesbury, 'He will, but they must have some food directly.'

He drove home, and instantly sent two churns of soup, enough to feed four hundred.

This caring attitude was not new, nor did it die with Shaftesbury. In 1586 Sir Philip Sidney was wounded at the battle of Zutphen and after a lingering agony died sixteen days later. While he was being carried back, there occurred an incident which highlights the upper class attitude to the lower orders under their command. 'Passing along by the rest of the army, where his uncle the general was, and being thirsty with excess of bleeding, he called for a drink, which was presently brought him; but as he was putting the bottle to his mouth he saw a poor soldier carried along who had eaten his last at the same feast, ghastly casting up his eyes at the bottle; which Sir Philip, perceiving, took it from his head before he drank, and delivered it to the poor man with these words: "Thy necessity is yet greater than mine." And when he had pledged this poor soldier, he was presently carried to Arnhem.'

The monarch and the upper class

The upper class have always considered that they owed their first service to the monarch. This is almost natural since they owe their origin as a class to the monarch; he created them, in return they owe him a debt of gratitude which can best be expressed in service. This close link between the throne and

31 Anthony Ashley Cooper, Lord Shaftesbury, the noted social reformer.

32 The first Duke of Wellington, a typical member of the upper class. A noted soldier and an opponent of political reform, Wellington was nonetheless prepared to give way to the demand for reform if it was sustained for long enough.

the upper class can be seen in reverse if we look at the fate of the upper class of some European countries. When the monarch of Russia was overthrown in 1917 there also disappeared, never to return, the Russian aristocracy. Once wealthy and powerful, many of them were reduced to abject poverty, earning their living as waiters and taxi-drivers in other European countries. When the monarchies of Spain, Austria and France disappeared so too did the political power of the aristocrats. When James I was asked by the English Puritans to agree to the further reformation of the Anglican Church and to the abolition of the office of Bishop, he replied, 'No Bishop, No King.' James saw that there was a close link between the Anglican Church and the throne and that any radical change in the one would lead to a radical change in the power of the other. The aristocracy equally could say: 'No throne, no aristocracy.'

The upper class have always served the monarch as soldiers. In the nineteenth century the Duke of Wellington had great influence over the army and over Ministers dealing with the army. The Duke, a third son of the Earl of Mornington, was a champion of the upper class. He had always favoured 'sprigs of the nobility' while he was in command and fervently believed that family and fortune should influence promotion. For the Duke and his class, it was not a question of what you knew but whom you knew – or to whom you were known. One of the signs of the

49

33 Strawberry Hill. Horace, the youngest son of Sir Robert Walpole, built this 'little Gothick castle' for himself and made it a centre of learning from 1747 onwards. His income came from public office as befitted the son of the man who thought that 'every man has his price'.

decline of the upper class can be seen in the reforms of the 1870s by which a middle class Minister, Cardwell, serving in a Liberal government led by a shipowner's son, Gladstone, got Parliament to pass a series of Acts which reformed the British Army.

The need for these reforms had been clearly indicated by the disasters of the Crimean War when the Army, led by Lords Raglan and Cardigan, had failed to inflict the expected defeats on the inefficient Russians. In the hope that a new, thrusting middle class officer class would be created and would in turn help to create a new Army, Cardwell abolished the old system by which commissions were bought and sold; in future promotion was to be by merit and not by influence.

How to get rich

The upper class had always served the monarch as Ministers and administrators. For many of them this was an opportunity for getting richer. In the eighteenth century the second Earl of Nottingham was a Secretary of State for four years during which he made £37,000 for himself – and this at a time when a labourer's wages were about five shillings a week. One of the most famous users of this system of personal enrichment while serving the monarch was Robert Walpole, who spent nearly £500,000 on building palaces and homes for himself while at the same time spending about £25,000 a year on personal expenses. James Brydges was the fourth son of an impoverished Herefordshire gentleman. Having been Paymaster General of the Forces, he made enough to build himself a palace at Canons – sufficiently large to back up his new title of Duke of Chandos, had £250,000 in various stocks and shares, and an income of £10,000 from rents off his estates.

Today we might think this a corrupt system. It is unlikely that any Minister would try to justify such money making. In the eighteenth century Walpole's son, Horace, drew a quarter of a million pounds from various government jobs and neither he nor his fellows thought this in any way wrong. Indeed, as Lord Clive said: 'I am amazed at my moderation'. Another Lord, Hardwicke, saw public office and its rewards as a sort of rich man's Poor Law system. He wrote: 'I look upon such pensions as a kind of obligation upon the Crown for the support of ancient noble families.'

While Cardwell was attacking the power of the upper class in the Army, so too was Gladstone's government attacking the opportunities of the upper class to make money out of the public purse. In a series of reforms in the 1850s and 1860s, entrance to and promotion inside the Civil Service was opened to a wider public by the establishment of a system of entrance and promotion examinations. In future the chance of getting a job in the Civil Service would depend on ability. This change marks a stage in the decline of the upper class. If they could not get their huge incomes from public office how were they to survive?

An independent class

It is worth noting that the upper class, while accepting that they had a duty to serve the monarch, also showed a spirit of independence which later politicians, from the middle class, dare not show. Such independence is the result of that early confidence which Prince Loewenstein wrote about. Unlike the thrusting, ambitious, climbing middle class, the upper class could afford to act with spirit. The Duke of Devonshire, a Cabinet Minister on several occasions, refused on three separate occasions to be Prime Minister. He was too involved with his estates and his dependants to take on the role of Prime Minister. On the other hand, the middle class politicians, like Disraeli, regarded the office of Prime Minister as the top of the 'Greasy Pole'.

Which modern middle class Prime Minister would speak to a monarch as Lord Melbourne did to Queen Victoria? When the Queen became engaged to Prince Albert, she wished him to be made King Consort by Act of Parliament, and urged her wish upon the Prime Minister, Lord Melbourne. At first that sagacious man simply evaded the point, but when her Majesty insisted on a categorical answer – 'I thought it my duty to be very plain with her. I said: "For God's sake, let's hear no more of it, ma'am; if you once get the English people into the way of making kings, you will get them into the way of unmaking them.'''

The upper class served the community in a variety of ways, but did not confuse such service with servility nor with any idea of voluntarily giving up their own social status and power. If they were good shepherds to the flocks they had no idea of themselves changing places with their sheep. While they accepted the obligations of *noblesse oblige*, they did not confuse this with the Christian beatitude which says that 'Blessed are the meek, for they shall inherit the land'. They knew that the land and its power belonged to the confident, arrogant, independent yet serving upper class.

34 Christmas celebrations in Stuart times.

6 Upper Class Enterprise

The English and Europeans compared

Unlike upper classes of other European countries, the English upper class has never failed to appreciate the value of money earned from industry, trade or political life. The Tudor *nouveau riche* had made their money in this way; their Stuart successors not only owed their elevation to the upper class to trade but continued, after their acceptance in that class, to try to add to their incomes by engaging in trade. One of the reasons for the unpopularity of the Stuart Kings was that they gave the upper-class favourites the monopoly in one or more forms of trade and industry, so that only the favoured few could earn the vast profits from the salt, the tea or the chemical trades. The English upper class did not consider such money 'filthy lucre' as did so many Europeans.

The English upper class was always a rural class, living in a country seat for many months in the year. The French and other continental upper classes were

35 Robert Devereux, the Earl of Essex, a favourite of the ageing Elizabeth I.

drawn to live at a Court, such as that of Versailles, where – near the King –they dawdled away an empty life of glittering tedium. The English upper class, on the other hand, while spending some of their time at Parliament and living for some time in London to enjoy the season of festivities, used the long Parliamentary holidays to return to their estates.

Enterprising farmers

In Tudor and Stuart times the more enterprising landowners were quick to see the opportunities to increase their incomes either by increasing the rents charged to their tenants or by farming large parts of their estates for themselves and using more efficient, productive and profitable methods of farming. In the eighteenth century there was a similar story. Not all English landowners took part in the development which has earned the title of Agrarian Revolution. Some were too old, others too uninterested in changing the traditional methods which had brought them wealth. But the changes that taken together made up that Agrarian Revolution were, in large part, the work of the upper classes. In the 1720s the Duke of Somerset took a keen interest in his tenants' farming and kept a notebook on matters of special interest. Sir Robert Walpole, although Prime Minister from

36 Charles Townshend, second Viscount, popularly known as Turnip Townshend.

37 In this painting of sheep shearing at Woburn, the Duke of Bedford is seated on horseback. He and many of his fellow noblemen, took a great interest in the new methods of farming.

1721 until 1742, always opened the letters from his steward or gamekeeper before reading the State papers. His brother-in-law, Lord Townshend, was not the first to use turnips, as his nickname seems to suggest, but he did extend their use on his estates and tried to make popular the four-course rotation method which helped to make farms both more productive and more profitable.

At Wentworth the Marquess of Rockingham farmed 2,000 acres himself, and was personally involved in experiments to see how lime and manure improved turnip yield. He had two model farms, one using Kentish methods and one using methods popular in Hertfordshire. Lord Howe wrote a paper for the Board of Agriculture's report on the West Riding; in 1722 Lord Sheffield founded at Lewes in Sussex a society for the 'encouragement of agriculture, manufacture and industry'.

A later generation of climbing middle classes would have shared the opinion of Gwendoline Fairfax who, in Oscar Wilde's *The Importance of Being Earnest* said that she was 'glad to say I have never seen a spade'. The rural upper class, however, was best represented by the Countess of Circumference in Evelyn Waugh's *Decline and Fall*. Her advice, 'dig it and dung it' echoing round the school sports field was a piece of down to earth advice which the upper classes would have understood. George III, giving the royal lead to his upper class followers, enjoyed his nickname of 'farmer George', while the Earl of Leicester (Coke of Holkham), the Duke of Bedford (at Woburn Abbey) and Lord Althorp were prominent in developing new and profitable methods of stockbreeding.

Urban developers

The upper class have always been landowners; this, after all, is what marked them off from the lower orders, and any member of those orders who amassed

55

enough money to warrant an attempt to climb aboard the upper class bus always realised that landowning was the hallmark of being 'upper', and paid his entry fee by buying an estate. In centuries gone by, parts of the landowner's estate were used mainly for agricultural purposes. But as towns expanded in the sixteenth and particularly in the nineteenth centuries, so these estates became more valuable as land on which houses, offices and shops could be built.

In 1826 the Lord Grosvenor (whose other family titles include the Dukedom of Westminster and the Viscountancy of Belgrave), got Parliament to pass an Act to allow him to exploit the building possibilities of his estate at what is now Belgravia. Not many people realise that as they walk around the shops of Grosvenor Place and the other parts of Belgravia that they are treading on the estate of one of the country's richest families, part of whose income comes from the rents they get from the valuable properties which they have built themselves or allowed other people to build on their land. In 1860 in Belgrave Square there lived three dukes, thirteen other noblemen and thirteen MPs each in his own vast establishment – most of which today serve as Embassies since the upper class is no longer as rich as it was and can no longer afford to maintain these huge establishments. But nobleman or Embassy, the income to the Grosvenor estates is the same – vast.

Such estate development has a long history. John Evelyn wrote in 1665 about the development of the Bloomsbury area by the Earl of Southampton. On the site now occupied by the British Museum the Duke of Montagu had a vast house, while the Bedford family's development of their estate can be traced in their family names which dominate part of this area – Russell, Tavistock, Bedford and Woburn are all remembered in Streets, Squares or Roads and all bring in the vast income required by the upper classes. They made their first development in 1775 when they built Bedford Square; now the once grand houses are the offices of architects and publishers. They also owned the Covent Garden area and from 1630 onwards they had begun to develop that area north of their own town house on the Strand.

Similar developments added to the incomes of families such as the Butes. While the Marquis lived in Cardiff Castle and watched that fishing village grow first

38 Eaton Square, Westminster. In 1826 a private Act of Parliament was passed to allow the Duke of Westminster to drain the area, raise the level and exploit the building possibilities. From this period date many of the squares which make London a beautiful city.

39 John Lambton, the first Earl of Durham, a leading member of the Radical wing of the Whig Party in the 1830s. He was the author of the Durham Report (1838–39) which was a major landmark in the development of a new attitude towards the colonies.

to a town then to a city, he also supervised the development of the land which he owned and on which he built, or allowed to be built, docks, railway stations, hotels, shopping centres and houses – all providing him with a rental of hundreds of thousands of pounds per year. The Durham family were similarly fortunate in that the Industrial Revolution's demand for coal could be satisfied only by the development of coal seams on their estates. The sort of income they enjoyed can be indicated by the statement made of 'radical' Lord Durham who, in the 1830s thought that a man could 'jog along on £40,000 a year' and this when the average workman earned about 50p per week. No wonder he was known after this as 'King Jog'.

This urban development which enriched the upper classes was the result of the industrial revolution which transformed the face of this country, changing it from a mainly agricultural country of small villages in 1800 to an industrial country of mainly large towns by 1900. While on the one hand this change brought great wealth to some upper class estate owners, it also spelt ruin for them in other ways as their power and position were challenged by a new rich middle class, while their agricultural interest was ruined by the importing of cheap, foreign food, after the 1870s. It was a mixed blessing.

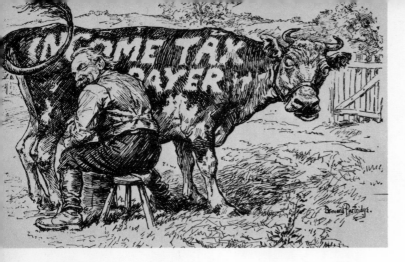

40 One view of Lloyd George as Chancellor of the Exchequer, 1909–15. As the government began to spend more on social welfare so the Chancellor had to increase the amount he collected in taxes. He increased the level of income tax to 1s 3d (6½p) in the £ – much to the annoyance of the income tax payers who thought that the country could not stand this level of taxation. We know better today.

This urban development enriched the urban estate owners who, like the Bute family, never sold the land to urban developers but merely leased it, charging an annual rent to the developer or occupier. This system of leaseholding meant that the upper class incomes continued to rise as rents rose and property on their urban estates became more valuable. But this increased value of their land was due to no work on their part; like their claim to a seat in the Lords this increased land value was due to historical accident. If the Industrial Revolution had not taken place, if London, Cardiff, Newcastle and other towns had not been built on the estates of the upper classes, then their incomes would not have risen in the way they did. This was why Lloyd George and other radical politicians began to tax the upper classes more heavily in the twentieth century than had been the case in the past. Death duties had to be paid by the heirs of estates when they inherited; income tax was increased and a new tax, called super tax, was imposed on people who enjoyed a high income. This heavy taxation was another reason for the decline of the upper class and many of the rich landowners were forced to sell off part, at least, of their estates. The Bute family sold the freehold of their Cardiff estates to the City of Cardiff; the Duke of Westminster has been forced to sell part of his London estates to property companies which, in one sense, have replaced the upper class as the country's landowners.

Industrialists

The upper class, while a rural class, has always been interested in the development of trade and industry. While one landowner, Raleigh, is popularly thought to have introduced tobacco into England, another landowner, the Marquis of Carmarthen in 1698 persuaded Peter the Great of Russia to give him the concession of importing Virginian tobacco into Russia. The Duke of Chandos developed oyster fishing for pearls off Anglesey, had shares in the Covent Garden playhouse and experimented in extracting precious metals from various ores in his own laboratory at Canons, his country seat. The second Duke of Montagu developed his estate at Beaulieu where there was an iron works in 1603, a forge hammer worked by a water wheel and which had a free harbour. He had also been granted the sugar islands of St Vincent and St Lucia in the West Indies and planned the building of a port on the Beaulieu river, including the building of a shipyard at Buckler's Hard, where, later, Nelson's *Agamemnon* was built.

In the eighteenth century the Duke of Bridgewater increased his income by about £40,000 a year by building a canal from his coal mines at Worsley to the developing town of Manchester. In 1773 the Earl of Thanet built the Skipton canal to carry lime and limestone from his estates. The Marquess of Stafford cut a canal to serve his ironworks in Shropshire. The development of the Welsh coal valleys owed a good deal to the Bute family whose name is commemorated in the Docks and estates in Cardiff bearing the family name. Few English landowners would have been as stupid or unenterprising as the Youssoupoff family in Russia who ignored the crude petroleum on their estates by the Caspian Sea.

41 The third Duke of Bridgewater portrayed with his famous canal.

Towards the end of the nineteenth century many of the upper class realised that vast fortunes were to be made out of developing the frontiers of the Empire. They used their contacts with businessmen for information and advice. Cecil Rhodes became a favourite guest at house parties. The English upper class became interested in Kenyan timber, South African diamonds, Mexican gold and Rhodesian copper. They entered into the upper-middle-class world of stocks and shares and after the onset of the agricultural depression of the 1870s the land-owning class tried to spread their assets by investment on the Stock Exchange. Many of them became directors of public companies; some, like the Earl of Warwick formed their own companies to run their own estates.

While this was happening a new, very rich middle class was growing politically more important and socially more ambitious. Edward, Prince of Wales, chose his friends from this new, pushing class, which made its money in finance, trade and industry (Chapter 7, Picture 44). For the first time in English history a rich class did not try to escape from its business origins by becoming landed aristocrats. On the contrary, the landed upper class tried to imitate the way of life of the new class although still pretending to despise the new, rich and vulgar.

Opportunities for the upper class are fewer in the twentieth century than ever before. Their landed estates are less valuable since 1870 than before – unless urban development allows a former piece of agricultural land to be developed as building land. Nor is there the opportunity today for a modern Duke of Bridgewater to make his mark and increase his fortune by an industrial development; today's industrial developments are too huge and expensive for any single individual to pay for; modern developments are paid for by public companies or by government agencies.

At the same time the upper class has fewer opportunities in Church or State to make the fortunes that came their way in the past while the democratic State takes away an ever-increasing part of their income in taxation. Some of the modern upper class have come to terms with this new society. Some, like Lord Lichfield (Chapter 10) have gone into that ultra-modern world of fashion and photography; others have opened boutiques or run pop groups. But the older, more stable members of this class are trying to develop their inheritance. Lions at Longleat, a circus at Woburn, are merely two of the more gimmicky ways in which the owners of the stately homes have tried to make their homes a source of income. In 1971 a 'school for stately home owners' was opened at the urging of the enterprising Lord Montagu of Beaulieu who believes that modern business methods should be applied to this business of running a stately home. He believes that there is a good deal of money to be made and even supports a move to start a tourist agency which advertises in phrases like: 'have breakfast with the Lord . . .' 'spend a day or two in the company and household of the Duke of . . .'. American and other tourists are willing to pay vast fees for the privilege of living like a Lord and with a Lord for a few days. Maybe the upper class are due to become a sort of housekeeping class for the rich industrialists of our new society.

7 Upper Class Entertainment

Throughout the centuries one of the distinguishing marks of the upper class was the size of their income, which in turn allowed them to spend huge sums of money on houses and furniture, clothes and food, servants and travel. People who enjoyed these huge incomes and whose families had always enjoyed similar incomes, became accustomed to spending money in what less wealthy, less assured people might consider to be an extravagant way. Equally an ambitious, pushing, self-improving middle class might consider that the upper class wasted a good deal of their time in 'leisure' whereas the confident upper class might echo the words of Prince Loewenstein's father (Chapter 5) 'Do? What is there to do?' So the upper class had to devise ways of spending not only money but time, and in so doing they provided the lower classes with examples of how to spend one's leisure time – examples which, in general, have been copied and are still being copied.

Rural sports

We saw in Chapter 3 that the English upper class was essentially a rural class, spending most of their time on their country estates. Naturally, then, most of their entertainment had to be found in the countryside. From medieval times they assumed that horses and hunting were a normal part of life. In Charles II's reign the upper class Parliament passed the Game Laws which prevented all freeholders of less than £100 a year – by far the great majority – from killing game (pheasants etc.) even on their own property; such sport was intended only for the very rich. A nobleman was prepared to spend a very high proportion of his income on blood-sports. Horses, hounds and hawks were bought and kept, a large staff had to be maintained to feed and equip the animals. In 1642 the Earl of Bedford spent only £230 on his Woburn stables, kennels and mews (for his

42 The Hunt, 1870. A popular but costly upper class entertainment.

birds), but as he got richer so his spending increased to £1,700 a year. This, of course, included everything that had to be bought – horse, hawk, dog, coach and chair, as well as the uniforms of the Gentleman of the Horse and his 15 stablemen.

Horse racing

In the nineteenth century many of the upper classes kept their own packs of hounds and a racing stables at Newmarket, and spent thousands a year on these alone. At the beginning of the century Lord Fitzwilliam's riding horses cost him £2,500 a year, his hounds £500 a year and his racing stables another £3,000 – and this while the workers in the cotton mills were earning less than ten shillings a week. The increasing popularity of shooting added to the cost of an estate; at Longleat, for example, the spending on raising pheasants rose from £264 in 1790 to £3,000 a year in the 1890s. For such an outlay one could expect to slaughter between 1,000 and 2,000 birds in a season. Foxhunting reached a peak of popularity in the 1860s, when there were 125 packs of hounds, many of them privately owned – as was the Belvoir pack which cost £2,000 a year.

Racing, prizefighting, hunting and cock-fighting were all supported by the upper class. In the eighteenth century a number of sports had been established which brought together people of all classes and helped to break down, for a short time each week, the class barriers. Cricket was established in 1774 under the noble hand of the Earl of Tankerville. Upper class landowners took their villagers to play against other villages and, as in most other activities, played for high stakes.

43 Baron Rolf Beck's Partridge Shoot at Brocket Park, Herts, October 1948. After a 12-mile shoot the party examine their victims.

44 Edward, Prince of Wales, dancing with fellow guests at a country house party. The two ladies in darker dresses were American heiresses married to English upper class husbands.

The Duke of Dorset tried to get good bowlers to come to work on his estate so that his team could defeat Lord Sandwich's team. The famous Hambledon club was organised by the Duke of Bolton's son to take on the rest of England.

Many of these activities have been copied in later times by the lower classes in England. Cricket, racing, hunting are no longer the perquisites of the upper class, while every ambitious middle class father and mother send their children to a riding school so that the children can acquire that upper class habit of horse riding.

House parties

Hunting and shooting were not sports which a man enjoyed in isolation; for these as for many other forms of sport the members of the upper class spent their time in each other's houses. This was a traditional upper class way of spending one's leisure time, as can be seen from the number of homes which advertise 'Queen Elizabeth slept here'. The Medieval and Tudor Courts travelled from noble place to noble place throughout the country and their upper class dependants soon learned to do the same. In 1713 Lord Fermanagh was writing to Ralph Verney – 'Deare Ralph – I am very glad Christmas is Ended, for we have had every day a vast number of people, but my servants say here were 400 people and I doe believe there were rather more last Tuesday, it has been a troublesome time; Every day with the noise of Either Drums, Trumpetts, Hautboys, Pipes or Fiddles, some days 400 Guests, very few under 100, that besides the vast expense it has been very tiresome. I wish all your family a happy New Year. This last night

45 The end of an evening's entertainment during the London season. A large town house, an army of servants and coachmen were essential features of upper class life in London.

a Fitt of the Gout tooke me in the Foot, which confines me to my Chaire for I can't goe about the room.'

Town season

Wives and daughters were forced to suffer the boredom of life in the country while their menfolk hunted and shot. In return, however, they were provided with a 'season' in London, which lasted for two or three months. A hectic round of balls and parties, shopping and entertainment which for the girl might end with the announcement of her engagement. Such a season might take several thousands a year. The cost of building a town house was at least as great as a country seat. The Lambs spent £100,000 on Melbourne House (later Albany), the Londonderrys spent £250,000 on Holdernesse House. When Northumberland House in the Strand was sold to the Board of Works in 1874 the family received

46 Sir Lawrence Dundas, with his grandson Lawrence, painted by Zoflany. Decorating the walls are some of the purchases of the upper-class owner who, in buying the paintings maintained the upper-class tradition of supporting the artist.

£497,000. Such palaces were for the very rich. Less wealthy members of the upper class had to put up with more modest houses. Lord Verulam paid only £13,000 for a house in Grosvenor Square in 1815. Others rented a house for the season, paying about £1,000 for a sizeable property in the West End. After paying the rent, the cost of the season depended on one's tastes in food, drink, servants and the rest. A modest season might cost about £1,000 in 1890 although the Earl of Newcastle spent £20,000.

Patronage of arts

The first members of the upper class – the medieval barons – had been, in general, energetic illiterates interested in fighting and hunting, with little if any interest in culture or the Arts. This had changed by the time of Queen Elizabeth I who presided over a Court which was deeply interested in literature, music and the theatre. The patronage of the upper class was very important for the theatre which reached a peak in this reign. Various members of the upper class adopted and maintained travelling companies of players; the first important one was the Earl of Leicester's, while Lord Strange, heir to the Earl of Derby had the famous Burbage in his company. Shakespeare's first plays were written for the Earl of Pembroke's company.

Other peers became interested in other art forms; some built up their own art galleries, buying such masterpieces as Leonardo da Vinci's *Madonna and Child* for £209 in 1863. Such galleries have, in later times, become part of the nation's collections as heirs have been forced to sell off part of their inheritance to pay for death duties imposed by unsympathetic governments. The upper classes commissioned portraits of themselves and their families and so helped to establish some artists; the Earl of Egremont launched Turner on his career by providing him with a studio at Petworth, and was a generous friend to Constable and others. This patronage was not confined to the artist and the playwright; poets, novelists and architects were also helped by members of the upper class. The system did not al-

65

ways work well; it would produce humiliation for the artists and bullying by a patron who demanded to be 'fed with soft dedication all day long' as Pope wrote of the first Earl of Halifax. But often the mixing of the worlds of society and art was of benefit to both sides.

The Grand Tour

The English upper class of the fifteenth century realised that their European friends were, in many ways, more cultured, better mannered, more polished than they were. They believed that such polish should be acquired by their sons. In later centuries the pushing middle class industrialists sent their children to the upper class public school, so that the rough Lancashire and Yorkshire accents and manners might be rubbed away in contact with the sons of the upper class. This was only an imitation of the behaviour of that very upper class which had sent its children into Europe in the hope that such travel might produce more cultured offspring. In the seventeenth century such a Grand Tour might take two or three years, during which the young man would acquire some fluency in modern languages and additionally some of the social graces, such as fencing, and dancing. Such travels were expensive; in the 1660s the Duke of Bedford sent his two sons on a tour which lasted six years and cost over £5,000.

In the eighteenth century this Grand Tour had become almost obligatory for the sons of the wealthy. In 1785 there were as many as 40,000 Englishmen and their servants travelling on the Continent. The Duke of Kingston spent ten years abroad on a Grand Tour which cost £40,000; most Tours lasted two to three years,

47 Fox, an outstanding politician as well as a noted gambler.

48 In 1951 Don Carlos de Besitequi threw a party at the Palazzo Labia, Venice. Members of the European upper class came to this extravangaza fancy dress ball. From England went Lady Duff Cooper (right) dressed as Cleopatra, her dress an exact copy of the Cleopatra portrayed in the ceiling above her.

at a cost of between £3,000 and £5,000 – but for the large familes of the period this would have to be repeated for three or four sons.

In the nineteenth century the rising ambitious middle class imitated their social superiors in all sorts of ways; they founded public schools for their sons, they bought landed estates, they tried to gatecrash into the London season. They even tried to organise a minor Grand Tour – but were unwilling or unable to afford to spend years away from their counting houses. They also lacked confidence; they were conscious of their 'newness' and of their lack of the social graces. To help them on their way Thomas Cook organised the first travel agency and took the first of the middle class tourists away from their factories to the culture centres of Greece and Italy. Since then, millions of the lower orders have taken advantage of their increasing wealth and the facility of foreign travel to tread in the footsteps of their social superiors. We are all tourists now.

The upper class spent extravagantly on their leisure pursuits. They also gambled huge sums of money – on their own horses or cricket teams, cards or the throw of a dice. In 1770 Lord Stavordale lost £11,000 at one sitting at Almack's, but was lucky enough to get it all back in one hand of cards. According to Horace Walpole, the diarest, he 'swore a great oath – "Now, if I had been playing deep, I might have won millions."' Such careless attitudes towards money could be shown only by those who were assured of an income and were accustomed to spending huge sums. Charles James Fox was not only a great politician; he was also a great gambler.

Cultured and yet boorish, patrons of the arts and of cock-fighting, hoarders of great pictures and inveterate gamblers, the upper class do not present a coherent picture of 'entertainment'. In our own time they no longer give the lead to the rest of society; they are today relatively poorer than they were and cannot afford to indulge themselves as once they did. However, they have done their work well and the lower orders follow the example which they once gave; we travel, visit art galleries, support local and national theatres, buy books, maintain libraries – and do much that formerly only the upper class could do.

8 Upper Class Children

The eldest son

What was it like to be a child born into an upper class home? The answer depends on which child you were and in which century you were born. Always, even today, the eldest son is a very privileged child because of the law of *primogeniture* under which the title, if any, and the estates all pass to him on the death of the father. The original reason for this law was that the medieval monarch wanted to be sure that his upper class followers would always be rich enough and strong enough to give him the support he needed – against internal disorder and against foreign enemies. If the estates had been split up between each child, or even between each son, in time an estate of a hundred thousand acres would have been split up – over three or four generations – into hundreds of postage stamp holdings, the owners of which would have been unable to afford horses, armour, the pay of soldiers and so on.

The younger sons had to be provided for in other ways. Some of them went into the professions – the Church, the Law or Medicine. Others went into trade. In

49 William Hogarth painted the Cholmondley children at play.

50 *Marriage à la mode*, by Hogarth, gives an indication of the size of the upper class house, as well as the bills that had to be paid after such a celebration (left-hand character). The young, rich man does not seem interested.

1812, R. L. Edgeworth noted: 'Church benefices may . . . be considered a fund for the provision of the younger sons of our gentry and nobles; and in this point of view, it cannot surely be a matter of complaint to any of the higher and middle classes in the community, that the clergy enjoy a large portion of the riches of the state.'

Marriage

For the younger sons there was left only the honour of being born to an upper class family; they then had to make their own way in the world. For the girls there was only marriage, with someone of their own standing if possible, and with some rich, climbing member of a lower class if necessary. Marriage settlements were a major part of upper class family history, involving property settlements, including dowries. These kept the lawyers busy. The sums of money involved can be seen from this letter written in 1736: 'Mr Joe Banks I hear has made his proposall to Miss Cassia. Lady Wray tells it so, they will be in town in a fortnight. Ten thousand down he desires, and twenty more at his death, which I think will just fetch him. We do nothing but marry and stuf ourselves with the turkey diet.'

Likewise, for the sons, marriage was an important part of the family life. The eldest son had to marry – in order that the family name should be carried on. If the family fortunes required it he might make an arranged marriage with a rich middle-class heiress – Sir Josiah Childe was a very wealthy East India merchant whose daughter was married off to become Duchess of Bedford. In the nineteenth century marriage between the English upper class and the rich American heiresses became quite common and the money of the New World was called to the rescue of the fading fortunes of the families of the Old World.

The education of the children was a constant source of parental concern. In medieval times the children of the upper class families were sent from family to noble family, living with their friends and relations so that they might acquire whatever graces were considered important. The boys learned to hunt and to hawk, to fish and to joust, to gamble and drink – while they served some upper class family as part-page, part-guest. The girls were sent on similar journeys or

51 Lady Randolph Churchill with her two sons, Winston (left) and John (right). Through his mother, Sir Winston Churchill claimed to be half-American.

52 The sons of the upper class while 'Absence' is called at Eton on their patronal day, 4 June. Their upper class parents wait to take their children out for the day.

to Court, and were expected to learn the female arts of proficiency at music, embroidery, waiting on the upper class males – and above all, the art of being caught by a potential husband.

Schools

Such 'apprenticeships' had to be paid for. In 1450 the Earl of Warwick charged £1,500 for taking in a page for four years. Academic education was paid for either by the employment of private tutors or by attendance at schools – in medieval times costing 2p per term in fees. At Winchester in the fifteenth century 3½p per week was charged by boarding houses for scholars' food and keep, while attendance at either of the Universities of Oxford or Cambridge might cost anything from the £6 spent by one of the Pastons in the 1470s to the £40 spent by a more riotously-living landed gentleman's son.

By 1661 the cost of education had risen. The Earl of Bedford sent his two younger sons to school at Westminster and paid £35 for their uniforms, £6 for two suits and £1·60 for shoes.

By the middle of the eighteenth century education was an increasing expense for the family. The sons of the landed gentry went to one or other of the four hundred or so grammar schools; but the nobleman's sons were educated either at home by a tutor or at one of the public schools before going on to University. A private tutor cost about £50 a year plus his board and lodging – not very different from costs in the seventeenth century. But the cost of University education had risen as the upper class children had acquired the careless attitude towards money which is one of the marks of their class. Lord Chandos' son spent over £400 a year at Oxford and similar sums were spent by boys at Eton. When we remember that this formal education was followed by the two or three years of the expensive Grand Tour we can see that education was a costly business.

In the nineteenth century the expense became even greater. The Industrial Revolution of the eighteenth and nineteenth centuries had helped to create a larger, more complex country requiring government by more educated and intelligent politicians and civil servants; a larger Empire required government by the English upper class. Education usually began at home, a tutor receiving £250 a year – and the tutor often followed his charges to their public schools where they paid £200 a year in tuition fees and board. This was followed by a year or two at the University at about £250 a year – so that the education of an average family of six children would come to about £1,500 or so a year. This was a charge that the upper class paid so that their children could be recognised and respected as educated, cultured members of the ruling, upper class.

Public schools

Life at the public schools was often brutal, as anyone who has read *Tom Brown's Schooldays* will know. Frederick Reynolds was at Eton when the boys revolted against the Head. His account of that revolution gives some idea of the attitudes of the upper class children of the early nineteenth century:

When I was at Eton, a circumstance occurred that threw the school first into confusion, and then into a rebellion. A boy in the sixth form, named Pigot, for some trifling offence given to Dr Foster, was flogged. This ignominious chastisement to one so high in scholastic rank, was deemed a perfect profanation; and the flame of discontent ran like lighting through the school. I can never forget the explosion of this diminutive rebellion; when, about two hundred boys, instead of marching into school, desperately rushed into the playing fields, and thence, threw about two hundred Homers into the Thames. It was the work of an instant, done as by the motion of the manual exercise; and never before did the greatest capacity imbibe Greek half so rapidly, as old Father Thames!

Having performed this noble feat, the two hundred rebels marched to the inn at Salthill, to refresh themselves, after their fatigues. The landlord seemed astonished at such a visitation; but did what he could to provide for his guests.

73

74   **53**   Upper class women and their partners riding in Hyde Park, 1872.

For myself, and forty others of the lower boys, accommodation was easily found, as we slept on the floor. In the morning, the reckoning came to one hundred and fifty pounds; but, this circumstance affected not me, for the best of all possible reasons – I had not a farthing. Recourse was, therefore, had to the late Duke of Rutland, and other boys of elevated rank, who, accordingly, suffered for their wealth. The result of the affair was that five of the ringleaders were expelled, and the rest returned home, to make peace with their parents.

Girls

The idea that the girls of these families should receive a similar sort of education did not become common until the middle of the nineteenth century and even then it was the girls of the middle class who benefited. Middle class women, who had failed to gain a husband began to demand an opportunity to take up a job – and needed education to fit them to do so. Middle class women like Miss Buss and Miss Beale founded day and boarding schools and Miss Emily Davies founded a College at Cambridge so that the girls, like the boys, could go to University; but this was not for the daughters of the upper class.

In this matter of education at boarding schools and university the upper class taught their middle class inferiors how to behave – as in so much else. The new Victorian rich middle class founded dozens of new boarding schools where their sons could receive an education which would, they hoped, make them little models of the sons of the upper class. By the end of the nineteenth century some of the new, rich upper middle class had managed to get their sons into the older boarding schools of Eton and Harrow.

The cost of education had risen throughout the nineteenth century, while, after 1870 the income of the upper class families tended to fall as the price of wheat and rents fell together. There were other attacks on the incomes of the upper class families – death duties, income tax and so on, while other costs – servants, housing and entertainment – were also rising. Faced with this situation the upper class started yet another fashion which later generations of inferiors have lavishly followed. They began to have smaller families so that the total cost of children's education could be kept within bounds even though the cost of each individual child's education might have to go on rising. The English upper class added a new dimension to the question of family size; to low death rate they added low birth rate – and the practice of birth prevention was introduced to England. The modern advocates of Pills and abortions have their roots in an upper class decision made in the 1870s to limit the size of their families. As their influence and position began to decline so, too, did the size of their families.

9 Upper Class Eccentrics

In the 1960s a pop-song was written poking fun at the way in which every American middle class family lived in 'ticky-tacky' houses which 'all looked just the same' while their children 'went to nursery' and other schools and they too came out and 'looked just the same'. This could also have been written, said and sung about the English, where the middle class males dress alike, live in similar mock-Georgian houses and take up the same fashions in food and drink, and where the working class, living on the sprawling council estates follow a similar pattern of life. Few, if any, of these people break out of the pattern of life which others have decided is fit for them and their class. Even the young, who seem to their

54 The Beatles in the early 1960s when they were the symbol of the youthful revolution in music, hairstyle and clothing.

elders to be rebels, are in fact, the greatest conformists – when 'minis' are 'in' all the young wear them. If 'they' decide that hair is to be long, then it is long; if sideburns are 'in' then everyone has to have them.

The upper class have always produced a number of men and women who have been ready to rebel against the conventions of society and to act independently. This is something which only the very confident can afford to do. One is reminded of the Duke of Wellington, when someone was trying to blackmail him with the threat that they would publish letters damaging to him. 'Publish and be damned' was the Duke's reply. He was not afraid of what society might think about him. The less confident middle class, eager to be accepted by society, unwilling to stand against the opinions of the majority of their fellows, have never been willing to stand up in this way.

The tenth Duke of Devonshire owned 200,000 acres and had an income of over £100,000; he could afford to turn down the offer of being Prime Minister – three times. While middle class politicians eagerly scramble until at last one of them reaches what Disraeli called 'the top of the greasy pole' and while those who fail write their autobiographies in terms of regret and of 'what might have been', the rich, confident and independent Devonshire considered that this high office was not worth his consideration.

They were even prepared to do things which more 'respectable' middle class people might consider 'beneath their dignity'. In his *History of Brighton*, Lewis Melville recalled the antics of upper class stagecoach drivers. There were in 1811 twenty-eight coaches on the road, and eleven years later no less than sixty, thirty going each way; on October 25, 1833, the coaches took down four hundred and eighty passengers.

Some amateur coachmen took the reins, some more or less regularly for a period. The Marquis of Worcester frequently drove the 'Beaufort', and the Hon. Frederick Jerningham 'tooted' the day-mail; while the prince of amateur whips, Sir St Vincent Cotton, had his own coach, the 'Age', with splendid horses and magnificent fittings, even the horse-cloths being edged with broad silver lace. The Cambridgeshire baronet . . . 'was as particular about the halfcrown "tip" as his professional brethren; and there is told an amusing story that when two old ladies objected to handing him the coin, protesting that they had known his mother, and he ought to be ashamed of asking for a fee, he retorted that if his mamma or his great grandmamma had ever patronised his coach, he should most assuredly have expected the usual "tip" from them.'

When next you listen to a modern politician explain away a mistake he has made – and try to show that he never ever made one at all, or when you are made to feel a fool because of a mistake made at mathematics, it might help to remember Lord Randolph Churchill, the son of the Duke of Marlborough. When he was Chancellor of the Exchequer in 1886 he made a series of mistakes in presenting figures to the House of Commons. When challenged about his errors he didn't try to show that he had never been wrong; he was not afraid to admit to being fal-

55 A stage coach in the early nineteenth century. Upper class riders often took over the reins of such coaches, racing against one another, from London to Brighton, for example.

lible. His simple explanation was: 'I never could make out what those damned dots meant'.

While the English upper class has been subjected to the same common law as the rest of us, unlike the French and Russian nobilities with their tax exemptions and legal immunities, some of them showed an arrogance which bordered on eccentricity. In 1760 Lord Ferrers was hung for the murder of his steward. There was the Duke of Somerset who had outriders to clear the roads of plebians lest they should see him as they passed. This arrogance was both born of great confidence and itself the parent of the same confidence. When Lord Brougham was staying with Lord Grey at Howick, Grey's grandson recalled: 'There is near Alnmouth (on the coast of Northumberland) a ford on the Aln which you may ride when the tide is not too high; one day my Grandfather, who had Brougham staying with him at Howick, proceeded to cross by this ford, when the marks by the river side indicated that it was rather doubtful if the crossing was safe. Half-way over, Lord Grey, who led the way, turned in his saddle and said:

"Brougham can you swim?"

56 Lord Randolph Churchill going against both political parties 1883.

Brougham replied:

"I have never swam, but have no doubt I could if I tried."

One is reminded of the man who, when he was asked whether he could play the fiddle, answered that he did not know because he had never made the attempt.'

Supremely confident of their own position, some of them behaved like the Macdonald of whom the following story was told in the 1820s: 'For many years . . . they were distinguished for a pride of spirit which seemed to disdain comparison with any state short of royalty itself. One of the lords, Macdonald, happening to be in Ireland, was invited to an entertainment given by the Lord Lieutenant. He chanced to be among the last in coming in, and sat himself down at the foot of the table near the door. The Lord Lieutenant asked him to sit beside him. Macdonald, who spoke little English, asked: "What says the carle [man]?" "He bids you move to the head of the table." "Tell the carle that Wherever Macdonald sits, THAT is the head of the table."'

If anyone challenged their position they got short shrift, as is indicated in this story about Wellington:

57 The first Lord Brougham and Vaux, a member of the Whig Government 1832–5.

'In dress the Duke was eccentric to a degree...Being much interested in animals, he once insisted on driving me down to the Crystal Palace, where a donkey show was being held. On our arrival there nothing would prevent him from walking on the especial piece of ground marked for 'For Judges Only' . . . He continued to stroll . . . when presently an official approached him and said:

"Sir, may I ask, are you a judge?"

"A judge of what?" thundered the Duke.

"Of donkeys," came the reply.

"Certainly I am, and [looking hard at the man] a very good one too; leave me alone." '

Until the end of the nineteenth century many of the upper class displayed their eccentricities in the way they spent their vast incomes. The Duke of Portland, for example, had a mile-long tunnel along which he could drive to his house unseen, and an underground suite of rooms to which dinner was sent down in a heated truck running along 150 yards of rail, while his riding school was lit by 4,000 gas jets. At his funeral there were 94 riderless horses attended by 50 grooms. When Lady Jebb stayed at Belvoir she found many examples of eccentric behaviour – peculiar servants with peculiar duties to perform, but none so strange as the watchmen, who frightened many a newcomer to death. 'There was a little of the watermen about them, but they were dreadfully silent and they padded. All night they walked the passages, terraces and battlements, yet no one really saw them . . . Always if one woke in the night, as the fire flickered to its death, one would hear a padded foot on the gravel outside and a voice, not loud enough to waken, but strong enough to reassure, saying "Past 12 o'clock. All's well." '

In modern England there is a tendency towards conformity in accent and speech. The middle class child goes to a boarding or grammar school and picks up an 'educated' accent so that, as Americans note, when an Englishman speaks you can tell where he was educated but not where he was born or brought up. The confident upper class used not to be so conforming. In the 1860s the Earl of Derby, the richest man in the country, had a broad Lancashire accent. Lord Palmerston, a great Foreign Secretary, displayed his contempt for affectation in speech and writing when he saw a French phrase used in a despatch sent by an ambassador. On the back of the despatch Palmerston wrote: 'Damn the fellow, tell him to write English or not at all.' Palmerston's 'damn the fellow' was in the tradition of the

58 Viscount Palmerston, the arrogant Foreign Secretary when Britain was the workshop of the world in the middle of the nineteenth century.

upper class who were not as mealy-mouthed as the more conforming, respectable middle class. In his *Collections and Recollections*, George Russell recalled: 'Men and women of the highest fashion swore like troopers; the Princes of the Blood, who carried down into the middle of the nineteenth century the courtly habits of their youth, setting the example. . . .' The Duke of Wellington's 'Twopenny damn' has become proverbial; and Sydney Smith neatly rebuked a similar propensity in Lord Melbourne by saying:

'Let us assume everybody and everyone to be damned and come to the point.'

The upper class were not likely to be overawed by anyone. When Beau Brummell was staying with his wife at Carlton House, the home of the Prince Regent, the Prince asked the Beau to ring the bell to call a servant. Brummell replied 'Your Royal Highness is close to it.' The Prince was very cross but, as Brummell explained,

'I was on such intimate terms with the Prince that if we had been alone I could without offence have asked him to ring the bell, but with a third person in the room I should never have done so – I knew him so well.'

In 1812 the Prince and Brummell finally quarrelled when Brummell and his friends gave a party to which, reluctantly, they agreed to invite the Prince. On

59 The Prince Regent about to enter a bathing machine at Brighton 1818.

60 Lord Melbourne, royal tutor and Prime Minister.

the evening the Prince appeared and Brummell and his three friends stood by to receive him. The Prince shook hands with one, Lord Alvaney, and another – Pierrepoint – and then passed by ignoring Brummell and the fourth friend, Sir Henry Mildway: The insult was deliberate – it was probably premeditated. Everyone present was horrified. A silence fell over the assembly. But Brummell was equal to the occasion. 'Alvaney,' he said quietly, but in a voice that penetrated the room, 'who's your fat friend?'

The upper classes had little respect for their royal superiors. On the other hand, the royal family had little respect for God. The Duke of Sussex, the Prince Regent's brother, has left his prayer book to posterity. In the margin of the book, opposite the Athanasian Creed, the Prince wrote: 'I don't believe a word of it.'

Today, a show of militancy by the lower orders seems sufficient to force the middle class rulers to change their policies – on wages, industrial relations or whatever. The upper class had more confidence in the rightness of their policies and of their abilities to govern. Of Lord Melbourne, Home Secretary in 1830, it has been written:

'. . . About the Reform Bill time, a deputation came to him at the Home Office (he was then Secretary of State for that Department) to urge that a procession should be allowed to march to the Houses of Parliament to present a monster petition. He pointed out that this would be against the law, and could not be permitted, on which the Deputation replied that, if force was used to stop the procession, it was to be feared that a riot might ensue. Lord Melbourne expressed his regret, but added:

"It is well, gentlemen, that you should know that, should there be rioting, the troops have orders to fire not upon the people, but upon you personally." No procession took place.'

Today there is a danger that a grey uniformity might spread over society as an increasing proportion of our people give up their regional accents, copy the manners and mannerisms of the 'respectable', live, dress and behave in a far too similar way. The eccentric may die out and we will have only memories of the ways in which some people once behaved – independently of the way in which 'the respectable' thought they should.

10 Where Did They Go To?

In George Orwell's *Animal Farm* the animals revolted against rule by the human upper class and, at first, established a society in which 'all animals are equal'. It was not long before the pigs had set themselves up as 'more equal than others' – and the animal kingdom had its own upper class. It seems that every society has had its upper class.

The British upper class owed their origin to the Norman King's need for a military class which would support him in foreign war and against internal rebellion. This class was rewarded with land – and its income. As we have seen, the membership of this class has changed as the centuries have rolled by, but always the upper class saw itself as one which served the monarch and the State, at the same time enriching itself as a reward for this service.

61 Servants' garrets in Cotton Hall, Denbigh. While the upper class family had their library, saloons, large and small dining rooms and so on their servants were crammed into the roof.

Reforming government

In the late nineteenth century this class and its ideas were beginning to lose their power. The task of governing an increasingly industrialised country was much too complex for a small group of amateur civil servants, relatives of the ruling upper class. In the 1850s and 1860s there was increasing demand for a reform of the civil service and by 1870 it had been reformed so that entrance into, and promotion inside, the service was governed by examination. No more would the upper class be able to take for themselves and their relatives the rich perquisites that had enabled a Walpole or a Cecil to enrich themselves and their descendants. From 1870 onwards the civil service became more and more professional, and its ranks were filled with the children of the new middle class – of industrialists, merchants and financiers.

The upper class had always provided the nation's military leaders. But in war, as in peace, things became more complicated in the nineteenth century, as new weapons were invented and new methods of transport and communication demanded a new approach from military leaders. The failure of the old-fashioned leaders to deal with the inefficient Russians during the Crimean War led to a demand for reform of the army, as sweeping as the reforms being carried out in the civil service. In the 1870s Gladstone's government proposed legislation which ended the practice of buying commissions; in future the army, as the civil service, would be led by people of ability.

Taxation and the upper class

In 1894 Sir William Harcourt, the Liberal Chancellor of the Exchequer, introduced a new method of taxation – death duties – as one means of paying for the increasing expenditure on education, slum clearance, and the poor. In 1909 Lloyd George, also a Liberal Chancellor, increased the rate of these taxes paid by rich men's heirs. In the past a man had been able to inherit from his father, increase his own wealth and hand it on to his descendants. After 1894, and more especially after 1909, the rich man's son had to hand over part of his inheritance to a government which was becoming increasingly active in social welfare, and so increasingly in need of more money.

Other taxes were also to rise in the twentieth century; income tax which had been 2d (1p) in the £ in 1880 became 1s 3d (6p) in the £ in 1909 and, in addition, Lloyd George introduced a new super-tax, on incomes over £5,000 a year. Employers also had to pay their share of Lloyd George's National Insurance Fund – while the insured workman paid his 4d (1½p) per week, the government and the employers also contributed another 5d (2p) towards the 9d (3½p) stamp which was stuck on the workman's insurance card and which paid for his unemployment benefit and medical treatment when sick.

The economy and the upper class

While the government was nibbling away at the wealth of the upper class, two other factors combined to lower the rate of growth of that wealth. Beginning in the early 1870s, Britain entered upon a period known as the 'Great Depression'. Britain had formerly been the world's leading industrial nation, her goods being sold almost everywhere and her financiers, businessmen and workpeople being the envy of the rest of the world. After the 1870s this was no longer so; the USA, Germany, France and Japan became industrialised competitors, depriving Britain of some of her export markets and even managing to sell their cheaper goods in Britain itself. The first industry to suffer in this way was agriculture; floods of American wheat, Argentinian beef, and New Zealand dairy produce poured into the country at prices which ruined British farmers – and their landlords. The upper classes found that their incomes fell drastically as the ruined tenants were unable to continue to pay the high rents charged during the prosperous years of the mid-nineteenth century.

Rising cost of living

But the expenditure of the upper classes and their families continued to expand – although their incomes were falling. Education became increasingly expensive, servants' wages rose, building costs increased. Many of the upper classes began to live on their capital – as their Tudor predecessors had done (Chapter 1). Some sold part or all of their estates to the new generation of rising middle class business men and financiers, eager – as this class had always been – to gather to itself the external trappings of respectability.

War and the upper class

But not even this new-rich class could hope to imitate the life style of their upper class predecessors, and as the twentieth century has gone on it has witnessed the

62 The burial of four British soldiers during the First World War. Many upper class families lost their sons in this war, while their fortunes came under attack from the increased taxation needed to pay for the war.

almost total decline of the old upper class and the failure or unwillingness of the new-rich class to replace the declining one. The First World War was responsible for the death of many of the sons of upper class families, for a steady increase in the rate of taxation and for a rise in the cost of maintaining town and country houses. That war also contributed to the growth of 'socialism'. The war was finally won because the country's leaders decided to use all the country's resources for an attack on the enemy. Men and women were conscripted for the services and for war-work, food and other essentials were rationed, government agencies were set up to deal with rationing, munitions productions, food distribution, soldiers' allowances, prices and wages. When the war was over there was a feeling among politicians, civil servants, radical writers and economists as well as ex-soldiers that the nation might do well to use its resources to fight against other enemies – poverty, sickness, unemployment, homelessness and so on. This feeling has continued to grow throughout this century so that taxation has continued to rise as governments have wanted more money to carry out those 'socialising' tasks which the nation has demanded. Supertax at one time reached the level of 97½p in the £ for anyone with an income over £20,000 a year; this meant that the rich man only retained 2½p of every pound he received over £20,000 a year. Income tax, death duties, petrol and purchase taxes, rising wages for servants who could earn high wages in industry or commerce, all have continued to make it almost impossible for anyone to maintain the life style of the old upper class.

63 Sir Alec Douglas Home resigned his title of Earl in order to become the leader of the Conservative Party and Prime Minister in 1963. By giving up his title, and seat, in the House of Lords, he acknowledged that the country could no longer be ruled by the Upper House. By resigning from the leadership of the Party in 1965 he acknowledged that the Party could not be led by a member of the upper class.

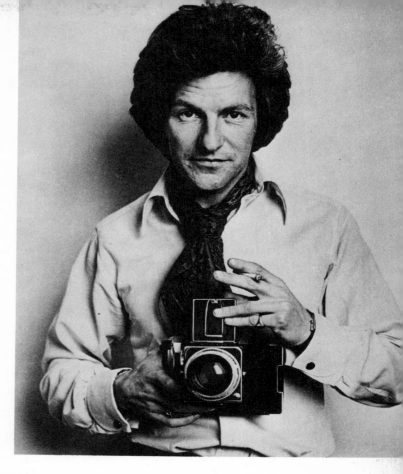

64 Lord Lichfield, a top fashion photographer.

The people and the upper class

In addition to these practical problems there has also been a change in people's attitudes towards the upper class. In the days when most people lived in small villages and towns, the lower classes accepted without question their place in the social structure; they accepted a society in which the men had to touch their caps and their women had to curtsy to the squire and his family. As we have seen (Chapter 5) this attitude was reinforced by the teaching of a Church which to the tune of *All Things Bright and Beautiful*, sang:

> The rich man in his castle, the poor man at his gate
> God made us high and lowly and ordered our estate.

Towards the end of the nineteenth century radicals of the middle and lower classes were questioning this state of society. 'They labour not, neither do they spin', said Joseph Chamberlain in his Liberal days. 'Of what use are these members of the upper classes?' was the question put by Radicals and Socalists. This antipathy towards the upper class has continued in what Sir Winston Churchill called the 'age of the common man'. When, in 1963, the Conservative Party chose the 14th Earl of Home as its leader – and so as Prime Minister – cartoonists, satirists, comedians (as well as serious political writers) thought that the Party had made a great mistake. Few people wondered whether the man had the capacity for the job; the choice was condemned simply because he was the 14th Earl of Home. No such attack was made on the Labour Party for having chosen Harold Wilson as its leader – although, as Lord Home pointed out, he was possibly the 14th Mr Wilson.

What to do?

The upper classes appear to have lost their reason for existence. The State does not automatically employ them as civil servants or military leaders; their incomes have fallen while the cost of maintaining their expansive life-style has risen. Some of them have retreated to their country homes where they try to keep up a leisured life style in the face of rising taxes and costs. Younger members of this class have joined the pop-set and taken some of the occupations which that set has created. Upper class boys and girls become dress designers, photographers, boutique owners, and the like. Some, like Lords Beaulieu and Bath, have used their homes and way of life as a business; their stately homes attract thousands of paying visitors each year. In 1970 the Duke of Bedford and others opened their homes to paying guests at about £100 for bed and breakfast; rich Americans and others can eat with the family, be wined and dined by the Duke and Duchess, who use the income to maintain their home.

65 A society ball, 1922. The upper class had once had a season in their own homes; in the twentieth century they have to take over one or other of London's larger hotels.

66 The Duke of Richmond (left) with the Duke of Northumberland (right) at Ascot. The noble lords are maintaining the traditional interest in racing. The Duke of Richmond is the owner of Goodwood racecourse.

Others of the upper class have entered wholeheartedly into the twentieth century, becoming successful business men and financiers. Men like John Wyndham (Lord Egremont), who have run an estate of 6,000 acres and the quarries and mines that go with the estate, fit quite easily into the world of business and politics – as he himself recalls in his witty autobiography *Wyndham and Women First*.

Their legacy

Perhaps their greatest contribution to the Britain of the twentieth century has been to hand on to their successors (in terms of wealth and industrial importance), some of the ideas of service and of social concern which have always characterised the best of the upper classes. The ruthless, climbing members of the industrial middle class created Manchester, Leeds, Bradford and the other horrors of the nineteenth century in their quest for profit. They had, as Asa Briggs points out, 'no social conscience, no civic pride'. If life in Britain in this century is more humane, one of the factors contributing towards the change has been the example of the old upper class. They have taught some of their successors some of their ideas.

Further Reading

First-hand information of upper class life can be read in:

The English Ruling Class, ed. W. L. Guttsmann (short accounts of a wide variety of aspects of upper class life).

The Creevy Papers

The Greville Memoirs

The Paston Letters

How They Lived (which has been issued in a number of volumes each of which includes extracts on upper class people and their life-style).

A History of Everyday Things in England, M. and C. Quennell

Tudor Economic Documents, Tawney and Power

A general survey of English History is an invaluable background to a study of the upper class. Readable and easily available are:

The English People, D. W. Brogan

The Establishment, ed. Hugh Thomas

Life in Norman England, O. G. Tomkieiff

Life in Medieval England, J. J. Bagley

Social Life in Early England, G. Barraclough

Medieval People, Eileen Power

Life in Tudor England, Penry Williams

Tudor England, S. T. Bindoff

Tudor England, G. Acton

Fifteenth Century England, P. Hunt

Life in Elizabethan England, A. J. Dodds

The Elizabethans at Home, G. Barton

Life in Stuart England, Maurice Ashley

The Century of Revolution 1603–1714, Christopher Hill

The Wealth of the Gentry 1540–1660, A. Simpson

Life in Georgian England, E. N. Williams

Life in Regency England, R. J. White

Life in Victorian England, W. J. Reader

The Portrait of an Age, G. M. Young

Life in Edwardian England, Robert Cecil

The Edwardians, V. Sackville-West

The Edwardians, J. B. Priestley

Studies in Social History, ed. J. H. Plumb

Biographies are a valuable aid to a study of the upper class. Most families have

produced at least one outstanding character whose life has been written up.
Good examples are:

Wellington, Elizabeth Longford
Roseberry, R. R. James
Sir Robert Walpole, J. H. Plumb
Young Melbourne, David Cecil
Lord M., David Cecil
Lord Salisbury, Kennedy

The *genealogy* which so interested Tudor upper class families can be studied in:

Burke's *Peerage*
Burke's *Landed Gentry*
Debrett
Heraldic Design, Heather Childs (which is also beautifully illustrated).

Upper class homes feature in:

Households of the Thirteenth Century, M. W. Labarge
The Town, Geoffrey Martin
Houses and Homes, M. W. Barley
Diary of William Taylor, Footman, 1837, ed. Dorothy Wise
Life below Stairs, Margaret Powell
The Victorian Household, Marion Lockhead
Inigo Jones, John Summerson
Robert Adam, Yarwood
Tudor Food and Pastimes, F. G. Emmison

Many houses have been written about in well illustrated books. One example is:

Holland House in Kensington, Derek Hudson

The upper class connection with the *armed service* is brought out in:

The Reason Why, C. Woodham Smith

The *landowning* aspect of upper class life is studied in:

The Land, John Higgs
English Landed Society in the Eighteenth Century, Mingay
English Landed Society in the Nineteenth Century, F. L. M. Thompson
The Agricultural Revolution 1750–1880, Chambers and Mingay
English Farming Past and Present, Lord Ernle

Apart from Burke and Debrett the *titles* of many upper class families are dealt with in:

Honours for Sale, G. MacMillan

American heiresses who married into upper class families feature in:

The Fabulous Leonard Jerome, Anita Leslie
Lord Randolph Churchill, R. R. James

The *political* activities of the upper classes are studied in a number of the books already quoted – particularly the biographies. In addition there are:

The Conservative Party from Peel to Churchill, Robert Blake
Lord Derby, Randolph Churchill

Lord Derby and Victorian Conservatism, W. D. Toms
Gladstone, Philip Magnus
Disraeli, Robert Blake
The Greasy Pole, R. Bevins

The *education* of the upper class is the subject of
Family Background of Etonians, D. Hall
Eton, Christopher Hollis
The Oppidans, Shane Leslie (just one of a number of good novels).

Some of the modern upper class have written their autobiographies. These include:
Old Men Forget, A. Duff Cooper (Lord Norwich)
Silver Plated Spoon, the Duke of Bedford
Before the Deluge, Sir Edward Cadogan
Men, Women and Things, The Duke of Portland
Noblesse oblige, Nancy Mitford
Wyndham and Children First, John Wyndham (Lord Egremont)

Conversations with living members of the upper class form part of:
The Last of the Best, Andrew Sinclair
The Aristocrats, Roy Perrott

Most of these books contain illustrations which will help those who are unable to visit any of the upper class homes now open to the public.

Index

The numerals in **bold type** refer to the pages on which illustrations appear.